HOME DECORATING
made simple

4 Easy Steps to Decorating Your Home Even If You Have No Time, Money, or Skills

Matthew Iacopelli

Adding live plants adds a necessary element in any successful home decorating project.

This book is dedicated to my wonderful wife Lynn;
without her support this book would not have been possible.

> "It's heaven when you find romance on your menu
> What a difference a day made
> And the difference is you."
>
> - Stanley Adams, lyrics from "What a Difference a Day Makes"

Copyright © 2016 Matthew Iacopelli

All rights reserved.

Natural lighting is beautiful in any space. Let the sun shine in your home whenever possible.

HOME DECORATING

made simple

4 Easy Steps to Decorating Your Home
Even If You Have No Time, Money, or Skills

Matthew Iacopelli

what's inside...
table of contents

Introduction – What You Will Overcome & Learn
1

Background – A Little About Me
5

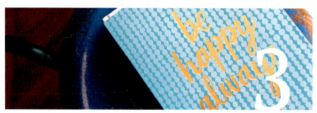
Changing Your Mindset About Home Decorating
11

The Home Decorating Success Roadmap
25

Step #1 Discover: Discovering Your Decorating Passion
29

Discovering Your Personal Style
35

Discovering the True Purpose of a Space
43

Simplifying For A Fresh Start
49

Making Home Decorating Goals & Plans
61

Step #2 Decorate: Creating the Backdrop of the Room
67

Creating a Color Scheme That Works
71

Decorating to Create Interesting Focal Points
89

Adding Style With Window Treatments
95

Finding, Creating, & Hanging Wall Decor
107

Step #3 Furnish: Adding Furniture and Furnishings
125

The 10 Commandments of Arranging Furniture
129

Choosing The Perfect Furniture
139

Repurposing The Furniture You Already Have
151

Thrift Ways to Save Money When Decorating
167

Step #4 Style: Finishing Touches & a Few Tweaks
177

Highlighting & Accenting a Space With Lighting
179

Styling Your Home With Meaningful Finishing Touches
185

Small Tweaks That Make a Big Difference
193

Putting It All Together
199

YOUR TWO FREE GIFTS

As a way of saying thank you for your purchase, I'm offering two free gifts that are exclusive to my book and blog readers.

First up is the one-page home decorating roadmap that outlines the entire book. This is a simple, beautiful, color PDF you can print off and hang somewhere in your house to help you remember the simple steps on your journey to decorating your home. It reinforces the 4 steps you will learn more about in this book.

Next is a free home decorating video series I have created for you. If you want to dive right into learning more about home decorating and discovering your style, then you'll want to grab this free video series!

To get your free gifts, go to:

DecoratingWithLess.com/bonus

CHAPTER ONE

Introduction

"Great things are not done by impulse, but by a series of small things brought together."
- Vincent Van Gogh

You can do this. You just need a simple steps approach that will guide you to decorating your home.

There was a time in the not-too-distant past when I struggled with home decorating. At times, despite being an interior designer myself, I felt that I would never have a well decorated home. With so little time and money how could I possibly decorate my home the way I want to, or the way I see in magazines, or do it for other people while working my day job. I would see small successes, but often I felt like I had more barriers keeping me from decorating my home. There are so many great ideas, before and after photos and advice out there that I was always confused on where to begin with my own home. However, I knew decorating my home was my passion because I was excited to work on creating a home for my family.

Nonetheless, I still had fears and worries that I would make a mistake. I questioned if it was worth the time and effort. I would say in my head, "my home will never look perfect, so why bother?" I also felt I didn't have what it took to decorate my home. I had so much doubt about picking anything for my home. I was too afraid to make a mistake that I felt paralyzed to even begin. I thought, why does it seem so easy for everyone else to decorate their homes, why can't I? Overall, the doubts, time, and money were the biggest barriers keeping me from making progress on creating a beautiful home.

You may feel like I did not too long ago. You are not alone. A majority of people struggle with decorating. Many of the people who visit my website, DecoratingWithLess.com, have told me they battle doubt and fear. Also like me, I hope you find comfort in the knowledge that you aren't the only one feeling insecure.

A Changing Point

The big changing point that has helped me make progress in decorating my home is changing my mindset about home decorating. I had some major realizations about home decorating and about what makes a house a home.

- I realized that perfection doesn't make a home beautiful.

- That decorating my home doesn't happen overnight.

- That my home won't look like the homes in magazines and on HGTV, because those homes aren't mine. My home will look beautiful because I am decorating it in my own unique style that is meaningful to my family.

These, and other realizations that we will discuss more about in Chapter 3, have helped me overcome my fears and obstacles about home decorating. My hope is by sharing how I came to this changing point I can help you discover a new mindset to apply to home decorating.

Who Is This Book For?

This book is for homeowners and renters, working and stay-at-home moms, singles and newlyweds, and anyone else that is looking to create a beautiful home that you can be proud of and showcase to your friends and family.

This book is also for anyone who has said to themselves:

- How can I afford to decorate my home the way I have always dreamed of?
- I don't know the first thing about decorating…
- How can I find the time or energy to work on decorating my home?
- How can my home look like the homes in decorating magazines and on Pinterest?
- How do I pick colors for my home that don't look terrible together?
- How do I get over my fear that I am going to make the wrong choices?
- How can I entertain in my home with my home looking like it does now?

If you have struggled with home decorating then you are in the right place. You have nothing to lose and so much to gain from discovering a simple roadmap to show you the steps to creating a meaningful home.

Decorating your home is a very fun and personal experience…that engages us physically, but also on an emotional level. Often, for many of us, the difficulties keeping us from decorating our homes…

…MONEY, TIME, KNOWLEDGE…are often the biggest obstacles.

I am here to get you through these barriers. Pure and simple.

…because decorating your home isn't just about picking colors. It's about creating an inviting and beautiful place to call home that enhances your life and all those that enter your home.

How do you decorate for the home you always wanted and get through those roadblocks in your way? You get started…TODAY!

Small steps today and everyday will help you get through those barriers that have kept you from having the home you are wanting. Take a sledgehammer to the brick walls in your way and finally get the home of your…DREAMS. You have everything it takes! You just need a simple roadmap to follow.

What's The Outcome

I know it stinks feeling helpless and lost when it comes to decorating your home. Our homes are a very personal and important place in our lives. A home provides us with shelter, but our homes are more than just a roof over our heads. They are a place where we make memories with the ones we love.

Since our homes play such an important part in our lives, it is no surprise we have such a desire to decorate them to reflect our personal style. My book will help you get past all of your barriers and feelings of doubt. The home decorating roadmap will guide you through each step of decorating a room in your home. You will feel confident and ready to start decorating your home because you will now have the tools, knowledge, and new mindset about home decorating.

You can do this! I am here with you every step of the way. Let's begin this journey…

I simply love the color of this nightstand at my uncle's house.

CHAPTER TWO

Growing Up, Theater, & A Major Turning Point

"Life is a journey. When we stop, things don't go right."
- Pope Francis

To help you get a better understanding of who I am, why I am passionate about interior design, and decorating on a limited budget, I have a story to tell you. It is a little long, but by the end of it you will know I walk the walk when it comes to creating homes on a small budget.

As a child, becoming an interior designer was not on my list of things I wanted to do when I grew up. I remember as a kid wanting to be an archeologist, probably because I was so fascinated by the Pyramids in Giza, who I am kidding I really just wanted a cool hat and whip like Indiana Jones. How did I end up growing up and becoming an interior designer? Well, we will get to that later.

Growing up I never lived in a home that I would call beautiful or a mansion, maybe out of date, but definitely not professionally designed. The first place I called home was an old farm house followed by two different 60's homes. We had old furniture, ugly curtains, and sponge painted walls. Not the home that would inspire a young kid to want to become an interior designer.

However, having a perfectly decorated home with the latest design trends was not priority for my parents. They had six hungry boys to feed. That's right I am the second oldest of six boys. I know what you are thinking, God bless my mom! Besides feeding us, my parents made it a priority that we all go to Catholic schools, which I am forever thankful for their sacrifices to send us to school where faith was at the center of education. Tuition was definitely a big expenses, but it was important to my parents.

My mom and dad also made family vacations a high priority. Typically we had one big family vacation each year, usually to my family's favorite destination...Walt Disney World. I have many fond memories of going to Disney with my family; the Tea Cups, Pirates of the Caribbean, The Haunted Mansion, and of course no trip to would be complete without many rides on the Monorail.

These are wonderful memories that I may have not had if my parents made having a big nice house a priority. To be honest, I am glad they chose family vacations over having nice furniture and a big house where I wouldn't have had to share a room with one of my brothers. Why? Because growing up I didn't care what my house looked like. I certainly didn't know what the latest home decor trend was or what expensive furniture looked like, but I did know I was loved by my parents because of the sacrifices they made to provide memories with their six sons.

My parents' love has made me a better husband, father, and person today; which is worth more than having a big home with new furniture and furnishings. You can't put a value on memories with those you love.

From Theater to Interior Design

As I said at the beginning, I never grew up wanting to be an interior designer and help others decorate their homes. Growing up I was always encouraged to follow my dreams and do what I love. Which is why before the thought of becoming an interior designer entered my mind I spent much of my adolescence and 4 years of college doing my first passion…theater.

I grew up going to see live theater with my parents at the local community theater in town. I was amazed by the shows and talent the actors had. Being in a show looked so much fun. I told my parents I wanted to be an actor like the people I saw on stage.

Starting in middle school, I began performing in school shows and auditioning for community theater. Now I feel so blessed that there is so much great theater in my hometown, however that meant there was a lot of competition to get casted in a show. Often I wouldn't get casted in a show, but I never let that discourage me, I just keep on going with determination that I would perform on stage.

My determination and hard work eventually paid off, I got casted in several small community shows. Eventually I would go on to get casted in shows at the big community theater too and even got the chance to perform in the touring production of *Joseph & The Amazing Technicolor Dreamcoat* for a week when it was in town. After that I truly caught the theater bug.

There Are Many Roles in Theater

Come high school, I came to the realization that I wasn't good enough to be an actor. However, I still had a passion for theater and lucky for me there are many ways to be a part of live theater without acting.

When I wouldn't get casted I started volunteering to work on the show as a crew member. This allowed me to have a great time helping create live theater. Though I wasn't on stage I still loved doing theater and it was still my passion. I got the opportunity to work most of the crew positions backstage, but my favorite backstage job was being the stage manager. The stage manager is the person in charge backstage during the show.

Theater was a great creative outlet for me and kept me out of trouble…mostly. I could bore you with stories from my theater days but let's fast forward a bit. In my senior year of college at theater school, I met a very special person that would eventually become my wife and best friend, Lynn. She was an accountant and business major, opposites do attract. After graduation she already had a job at a CPA firm in town while my plan after graduation was to head off to NYC to pursue a career as a professional stagehand.

Realizing that Lynn was the one for me and that I wanted to spend the rest of my life with her. I started rethinking my post graduation plans and career path. I discovered that new path during a scenic design class the semester before graduation. Scenic design is like interior design just for the stage. When I discovered my passion for designing spaces, I thought this is the perfect creative outlet for me.

I finished my degree in technical theater and then in the fall started going to school for interior design. I found a passion that would keep me near Lynn and we would have the same schedules. It was great! We got married during my second year of design school.

Theater lead me to a passion for creating beautiful homes for people just like yourself. It was a crazy path to realizing my passion for home decorating, it could have been easier if I discovered this before going to theater school, however, I wouldn't change anything for a second. The path I took to becoming an interior designer was just the right way God wanted me to go. I have never looked back since and I am so blessed.

Major Turning Point

I have made a lot of mistakes in my life. However, I have very few regrets about the mistakes I made because with every mistake or struggle I believe there is a life lesson to be learned. I also believe our mistakes can shape us into a better person, especially if we can see the lesson and change as a result. One aspect of my life that has always been a struggle is finances and debt.

When I was younger, in high school, I was typically very responsible with money. I started working when I was 13 in my parish rectory and always had a job of some sort. I'd spend some of my money, but usually some of my pay check always went to savings. My spending habits, however, began to change over time as I got older.

Using credit cards, student loans to pay for classes but also to pay off non school related expenses, buying a house bigger than we could afford, moving cross country with little to no money, and many other poor money decisions, my wife and I found ourselves in a huge amount of debt. Including the house at one time we had $200,000 in debt. We were drowning in debt.

We did our best to work hard to pay down our debts. We took Dave Ramsey's Financial Peace University, which motivated us for awhile, but we always would find ourselves back in the same poor spending habits. Eventually after getting one car repossed, nearly losing our house to foreclosure, and hating our phones because the only people calling us were creditors, we hit our breaking point.

Hit the Breaking Point

After trying to use debt consolidation services and a whole lot of praying, we declared bankruptcy. It was our only option. One we should have done two years earlier. Bankruptcy was our only hope to getting a second chance on life and get forgiveness for all the stupid mistakes and poor decisions.

Declaring bankruptcy stinks, however it has forced us to do what we never could do ourselves; get our spending habits in control and start living on less than we make. Now we're living, for the most part, on my income alone. My wife's income goes towards savings and to pay off debts that were not included in the bankruptcy. We are now on the path to financial recovery.

Why do I share this embarrassing detail about my life? Simple, bankruptcy has lead me to live more frugally and be smart with the money we have. I was also inspired to start writing about thrifty home decorating and money saving tips, which I do on my blog DecoratingWithLess.com.

Everything that I have learned from being frugal and saving money on home decorating has lead me to write this book. I want to share my simplified decorating process and home decorating savings tips with you. I know many people struggle with money, maybe not to my extent. So I know this information is needed and wanted. I want to show you it is possible to decorate on any budget. I know that is truth because I am on a shoestring decorating budget. It can be done and I will show you how throughout this book.

Now that you know a lot more about how I grew up, discovered my passion for interior design and the major turning point that has lead me here; let's jump into the foundations of my simple approach to home decorating.

This is such a beautiful room with a great view. The natural light is what really makes this room shine.

CHAPTER THREE

Changing Your Mindset About Home Decorating

"I think anything is possible if you have the mindset and the will and desire to do it and put the time in."
- Roger Clemens

It is so exciting to move into a new place. Instantly you begin dreaming of the million possibilities of this new home. You just can't wait to get started. You start picking paint colors, hanging art on the walls, buying home accessories and moving furniture around. You have so much momentum you know you can create your dream home.

Since my wife and I have been married, nine years, we have moved into eight new places. So almost once a year. At each new place I wanted to decorate so it would feel more like home. Each new place was a blank slate that I wanted to transform overnight into a showcase that was sure to get photographed for HGTV Magazine.

Most of the time, who I am kidding, all of the time, I failed to reach my goal. Something always stopped me from what I thought home decorating success meant at the time. Now I realize that my mindset for home decorating came from what I saw in magazines, HGTV, and on blogs.

Our outside world, TV, social media, and books or magazines give us a false impression of successful home decorating. I believed that home decorating had to be perfect and that perfection should happen overnight. I thought the only way of creating a beautiful home was by spending a lot of money on new furniture and home accessories.

The reality as I would realize and finally accept as true years later is home decorating takes time, doesn't need to be perfect, or cost me a ton of money. My mindset had shifted from the illusion I believed for so many years. Now I felt I could finally really succeed in home decorating.

Now let's dive into these myths of home decorating that cause us to struggle. It is important to start with a new foundation of beliefs and mindsets before starting so we can succeed where we once struggled or failed. I hope I can help you change your mindset so you have a fresh perspective of home decorating.

Myth #1 - I Don't Have What It Takes to Decorate My Home

You have a strong desire to decorate your home. I am sure you have even imagined the outcome and your family and friends' reactions in your head a few times. How amazing your home will look after you finish decorating each room the way you have always dreamed of.

However, there is something that is stopping you from taking the steps to creating a beautiful home. What's stopping you is you have a belief that you don't have what it takes to decorate your home.

Let me share a little secret with you, everyone feels this way in the beginning. I feel this way ALL the time.

I question if I am making the right choices and second guess every step along the way. But there is a way to overcome this thought…

Overcoming this belief all starts with a change in mindset. Instead of fearing decorating your home because you are worried you are going to make a mistake, decide to have confidence that you have what it takes to decorate your home.

Changing Your Mindset

You are probably saying, "that's a big change in mindset, Matthew." But please trust me that if you choose to have confidence that you can decorate and tell yourself that everyday, you will find decorating your home easier to do.

As internationally acclaimed speaker, trainer and coach Paul Martinelli says:

> *"Do it afraid, jump and build wings on the way down."*

I recognize that this may be hard to do at first, but let me ask you these questions.

- Is having a beautiful home worth changing your mindset?

- Will decorating your home make you happier and more fulfilled?
- Will your family and friends benefit from decorating your home?

If you said yes to any of those questions, then changing your mindset is worth it. Decorate in fear at first but just get started with something small that you have the confidence to do.

Maybe something small is to finally paint your living room. Taking small steps and having little wins at first will build on your level of confidence. Then, overtime, you will have the mindset to take on bigger projects that you once didn't have the confidence to do.

Your Talents Will Blossom

Here is a quote I found which I think applies to the myth that you don't have what it takes to decorate.

> "Any human anywhere will blossom in a hundred unexpected talents and capacities simply by being given the opportunity to do so."
>
> - Doris Lessing, attributed, Wisdom for the Soul

By choosing to have confidence in yourself instead of doubt, you are giving yourself the opportunity to discover and grow in your capabilities of decorating.

Everyone has the undiscovered ability to decorate...**that's you too**. I am virtually pointing at you and telling you that you have what it takes to decorate your home.

Believe you can do it, take small steps, and most of all have confidence that you have what it takes. If you get stuck or make a mistake along the way it is not the end of the world. Dust yourself off and keep on going. Let me tell you another little secret, everyone makes mistakes when decorating. Have the confidence that most home decorating mistakes are fixable.

If you get really stuck email me and ask for help. I want to see you succeed because I believe you can.

Our homes are probably the most important place in our lives. So it is worth all the blood, sweat, tears and changing our mindset to have confidence to create a beautiful home. You can do this!

Myth #2 - Perfection is Beautiful

Do you ever feel pressured to have a perfectly decorated and organized home? I know I do, especially as an interior designer! My home is a work in progress which yours may be as well. I like to say that home decorating is a journey and not a destination.

Why?

Why do we put so much pressure on ourselves? Is it because we won't find happiness until our home looks like the homes in the decorating magazines? Or do we think if we don't have this "perfect" home when people come over they are going to judge us because things aren't put away and organized, and ready for the perfect picture?

Whatever the reasoning is for you, I believe this pressure is unwarranted and needs to stop. Perfection is not possible nor does it guarantee a beautiful home. I believe when we are striving for perfection all of the time we are missing out on what is truly important in life…living in the moment and rejoicing in the imperfection of life.

Perfection Reduced My Confidence

Let me tell you a quick story, when we first moved back into our house I was so excited to get started redecorating and finally make the "perfect" home. However, I lacked the confidence to get started. I found that despite my experience designing interiors for other people, I was constantly second guessing myself when it came to my own home. My desire for "perfect" was reducing my confidence and creating fear.

I finally got over wanting to create the "perfect home" and instead I am working on creating an imperfect home. A home doesn't have to be perfect to be beautiful, after all, and done is better than perfect.

This my fireplace reading area in my home. It is not perfect, but we love! It is cozy and works great.

Thanks to The Nesting Place

My change in mindset, which gave me the confidence to get started, was in large part because of my reading Myquillyn Smith's book *The Nesting Place*. Myquillyn helped me get over my desire for perfect and instead see the beauty and simplicity of creating an imperfect home. Reading her book restored my confidence that I needed to decorate my home.

If you think your house has to be perfect I highly recommend you put *The Nesting*

Place on your read list to help you find peace in imperfection.

Instead of shooting to decorate a perfect home I challenge you to rejoice in imperfection and strive to create a real-life home. Those homes in magazines are not reality, they are real homes, but the way they look is not reality for most people, which I say is ok. Most of those homes may have been a disaster hours before the photo shoot and then were quickly staged for the perfect shot for the magazine cover. This is kind of like airbrushing for homes.

What Does a Real-Life Home Look Like?

Real-life homes are beautiful, too. You probably already live in a real-life home…I know I do. Creating a real-life home is all about embracing the imperfections of life. Real-life homes often have areas that are disorganized and messy at times, and that is okay.

These perfect homes in magazines and on television that make us feel bad if our home doesn't look like them, don't looked lived in. If someone came into one of these homes they may find them pleasing to the eye, but would they know anything about the people who call that place home? Probably not.

Real-life homes tell a story. They are meaningful and have more life than the staged photos in a magazine. When someone walks into my home I don't care if things aren't perfectly decorated and organized. I want them to notice the meaningful things that show that we love each other...such as the toys or art supplies strewn around the house because that means we are having fun together.

Permission to be Imperfect

Life is too short to sweat the little imperfections in life. Give yourself permission to enjoy and live life in the moment whether things are perfect or not.

This wingback chair was my wife's grandma's, even though the upholstery is worn it is still beautiful and a meaningful piece of furniture in our living room.

Stop thinking people are going to judge you because your home is not perfectly decorated. There are bigger things to be worried about than making sure all your home furnishings are perfectly placed and that your home matches the latest design trends.

Home decorating is a journey and a process that takes time to complete. Make your journey a meaningful one that rejoices in imperfections because it is those imperfect details that make your home unique and special to you and your family.

Myth #3 - Home Decorating is a Fast Process

There is an illusion, thanks to home decorating TV shows, Pinterest, and bloggers, that decorating is an easy and fast process. That overnight you can transform your house into a perfectly decorated photo-shoot ready home.

I am sure you are like me and you love watching HGTV, spending time searching through Pinterest for your next DIY project, and drooling over bloggers showcasing their beautiful homes.

Over time we believe the illusion that decorating a home is a fast process. I often hear from homeowners that believe this mindset. Many of them are my friends and clients.

They tell me they don't have the time or money to quickly flip their homes overnight into a beautifully styled home. They are too busy running errands, making dinner, taking kids to lessons, and keeping their home somewhat clean to get one second to work on decorating their home.

As I said before I had this mindset too. I believed I could quickly decorate my home into the perfect paradise. However, eventually over time and after a lot of disappointment that my home didn't look like the homes on TV or Pinterest. I realized that decorating is not a fast process and I can take my time, and as long as it took, to decorate my home.

What Happens When You Decorate Fast

When you decorate your home fast, it can often lead to making mistakes, spending a lot more money, and a home that doesn't reflect your personal style.

Let's be honest, most of us don't have the budget to go out and furnish our entire home with new decor quickly, which I see as a blessing. Even if we did, I believe that going out to a home decor store and buying everything for a room all at once leads to a space that doesn't reflect you.

Creating a meaningful home that reflects you and tells a story takes time to design. Going fast leads to a home that more reflects your likes from a moment in your life or looks more like a showroom than a home. Your personal style will change over time.

If I had the money when we first bought our home to completely furnish it quickly, I probably would have ended up with a ton of modern furniture and accessories. This would have been nice then, but now that I am older my style has evolved and modern design does not fit into my lifestyle with children. Now I would describe my style as more *Beachy Country Chic*.

If I spent all my budget quickly buying new decor and furnishings I would have regretted my decisions. I would be stuck with that decor for awhile since I spent a bunch of money and felt like I couldn't justify spending more money until I got my money's worth out of it.

Decorating Your Home is a Marathon

The better way to look at decorating your home is not as a fast sprint… but more as a slow and steady marathon. Decorating is a slow process that takes time as you collect, add, purge, search for bargains, thrift and repurpose items along the way. This process results in a home that is curated with love and amazing memories.

When someone walks into your home, your decor and furnishings should tell them a story about yourself and your family. If you decorate fast with accessories from XYZ Home Store, those items won't tell the right story.

The Awesome Benefits of Decorating Slow

I will be honest with you, I sometimes have trouble decorating slowly. It is not the easiest thing to do because we all want to be able to take the pretty picture to post on Facebook for all to see.

However, I promise, patience when decorating a home is worth it. There are many benefits to decorating slowly and over time verses the quick approach.

- **Save More Money** - Decorating slowly allows you to save money because you have more time to hunt for good deals or have time to makeover an old piece of furniture.

- **You Don't Have to Settle** - Decorating fast may mean you have to settle for a sofa, artwork, etc. that isn't exactly what you are looking for. When you decorate slowly you have time to find or create the right home furnishings.

- **You Get to Discover the Style You Really Love** - Like I said earlier, if I had been able to run out to my local retailer, I would be stuck with modern furniture. But now since I am on this slow journey to decorate my home I am able to discover the things that I truly love and are functional for my family. An Eames Lounge is beautiful and I would love to have one, but it would probably get destroyed by one of my daughters or dogs.

- **You Get More Creative** - When you are on a budget and decorating one layer at a time as you can afford it, you will find yourself being more creative with the things you do have. You discover that what you have does work and something new is not needed. There can be a greater sense of gratification when decorating slowly.

- **Mistakes are Easy to Fix** - Mistakes in decorating are a fact of life. You and I will make decorating mistakes. When decorating slowly these mistakes are easy to fix because you have saved money along the way. You can buy more paint or a different piece of thrift store art.

- **You Learn More by Going Slow** - By decorating slowly you will become a better decorator because you will take more risks, try new things, and learn from trial and error.

- **It is More Fun** - Rushing to do something is never fun. We have all felt rushed to get something done. You have felt rushed to cook dinner, read a book, or spend time with your kids. When you are rushing even things you enjoy doing are no fun. Decorating done fast is stressful and far from fun. Slowing down will make home decorating more fun because you won't be so stressed to finish.

- **Your Home Will Become a Reflection of You & Your Family** - Decorating your home over time will allow you the opportunity to furnish your home with more meaningful items. Such as the dresser from your childhood home that your grandpa passed on to you and is now in your child's bedroom. Or decorating your fireplace with accessories you found on a family vacation. Think of your decorating as the pen a writer uses to write a novel. The furniture and furnishings will, over time, create a story you can tell to your friends and family.

Creating a Beautiful Home is a Journey

I challenge you to take time decorating your home and change the mindset that decorating is a fast process. Instead of believing in the illusion, go on a journey that transforms your home into a more lovely environment for your family.

The journey may not always be easy but the results and benefits are huge when you arrive at your destination...

...a home that you will fall in love with and cherish for years to come.

Myth #4 - Home Decorating Costs A Lot of Money

How much do you think you have to spend to makeover a room? $5000, $10,000, $20,000 or more? You could easily spend that much money decorating a room, by you don't have to. Home decorating does not have to cost a lot of money.

I know money is often the biggest barrier people run into when decorating. I often hear, "I would love to decorate my home but I don't have enough money to start." As a result, they never start. You may have said this to yourself too, I admit I have.

Many people think they need to do everything at once. Meaning spending a bunch of money right away. Most of us don't have a pile of money set aside just waiting for us to start decorating. If you do, then what are you waiting for? But for the rest of us, myself included, it would be difficult, without taking on debt, to purchase everything at once for our homes. I never recommend financing the decorating of your home.

Why My Decorating Budget is Limited

At the beginning of this book I told you about my debt problems. A limited budget led me to be extremely passionate about frugal home decorating. I want a beautifully decorated home but unfortunately, because of my bad money decisions earlier life, I don't have the luxury to budget much toward decorating my home.

Currently I only have *$15 per month budgeted for home decorating.* This does not go far when it comes to designing a home's interior. However, I am grateful for what I have and use my teeny-tiny budget creatively to stretch each dollar.

Solutions to the Myth that Home Decorating Costs a Lot of Money

Decorating can cost as little or as much as you want it to. I believe, because I am doing it everyday, that you can decorate your home and make it look beautiful for far less than you may believe. There are three keys factors to decorating for less and proving decorating does not cost a lot.

You Have to be More Creative - It is time to think creatively because to make decorating not cost so much you have to make your own home accessories, refinish furniture, repurpose items as decor, and think outside-the-box when it comes to what you need to furnish your home.

You maybe saying, "but Matthew I don't have a creative bone in my body." I would say that is not true, because if you have a desire to decorate your home, you have creativity hiding somewhere within you.

Decorating with Less Stuff - Don't feel like you need to buy so much stuff. You don't need to have decorative owls or five pillows on the sofa. You can furnish your home more simply and it will still look beautiful. Furnish your home with only things you need to fit the purpose of the space. Over-furnishing your home is a home decorating no-no. Your home, I promise, will look more appealing with fewer furnishings, which I will talk about more in a later chapter.

Get Thrifty - One of the best ways to make decorating cost less is by being thrifty. What does this mean you have to do? To save money and help bring the cost of decorating down it is time to search for good deals that you can't find at the big box home decor stores. Your new favorite places to shop are thrift stores, Dollar Tree, garage sales, Facebook garage sale groups, street curbs, flea markets and clearance sections. At these places you can find amazing savings and you will be surprised what you can find on the cheap.

I made this ring dish for my wife that is not only function but also a beautiful accent in our bathroom...cost $3. Everything for this DIY came from Goodwill.

My wife loves finding the best deals on groceries, I love finding the best deals on home decor. After successfully scoring your first big savings find you will be hooked by the thrifty bug like I am.

In the Chapter 19, *Thrifty Ways to Save Money When Decorating*, I will talk more about steps to help you save on furnishing your home.

Home decorating with a limited budget is not always easy, but it is possible. So don't let the myth that home decorating costs a lot money stop you from creating a beautiful home. If I can make progress decorating my home on a $15 per month budget, then surely it is possible to decorate your home on any budget. Don't let money stop you from your dreams, because achieving them is worth it.

A neutral sofa is a perfect background to accessories with accent pillows.

CHAPTER FOUR

The Home Decorating Success Roadmap

"All you need is the plan, the road map, and the courage to press on to your destination."
- Earl Nightingale

Thank goodness for GPS because before I had it I would always get lost. Quick story, a while back before I went to school for interior design, I worked for an event ticket sales company. It was my job to drive around to all the ticket sales outlets in my area to support any technical issues and bring more supplies. I enjoyed this job because I got out of the office and wasn't stuck at my desk all day.

One day when I was out on my route to some new outlets, I got lost. I had printed off maps from MapQuest, but somewhere I made a wrong turn and I had no clue where I was. With no GPS or Siri to tell where go and to recalculate my route, I was helpless. Thankfully, I was able to get ahold of my wife, tell her where I was, and she was able to get me back on track.

If I had GPS back then I would have had no problem finding my way even if I made a wrong turn. The reason I am telling you this story is that with home decorating there is no GPS to give you step-by-step directions on how to decorate your home. There is not even a roadmap you can print off to guide you. So it can be very easy to get lost and not know what to do next.

Here is Your Roadmap

I have had the fortunate opportunity to design the interiors for many projects big and small over the years. Each project and each homeowner has its own unique needs, problems to solve and design. However, I began to notice I followed the same steps for each project. I also discovered that the decorating process works best when it is followed from beginning to end.

I have organized the process into 4 main steps that I follow when decorating for myself and others. In this workflow I have incorporated what works best as a result of lessons learned and mistakes made along the way to break down into a proven roadmap that you can follow to make home decorating easier.

We all want to find the easiest path to success…this path will help you get there. I will say, these steps work best if you work them. You may be skeptical that home decorating can be easy, but I am proof. I use this roadmap with my clients and in my own home. It can work for you, too.

You can take this roadmap and go as fast or as slow through it as you want. We are all busy with work and family. So you can start decorating and then work on it as time allows. As you read earlier, home decorating is a slow process. Doing a little bit at a time and over time will lead you to successful home decorating.

Will this journey always be easy…no. However, it is all worth it to have a home you are excited to invite people over to with no fears of judgement. This can be done by finding moments where you can spend time discovering, decorating, furnishing and styling your home.

My goal is to help make home decorating easier and less confusing for you. So I have incorporated the steps I take when decorating any project and designed a colorful one-page roadmap. This guide will help you know where to start and what to do next each time you decorate. Not knowing where to begin is a reason many people don't start decorating. This roadmap helps you get started and keeps you going to a successful destination…a beautiful home.

If you want to print off the *Home Decorating Success Roadmap*, I've made one available to you as a thank you for grabbing a copy of this book. Just go to: DecoratingWithLess.com/book.

The 4 Main Steps of the Home Decorating Success Roadmap

I have divided the 15 actions into 4 Steps; **Discover, Decorate, Furnish, & Style**. Each tier builds upon the skills you learned and is designed to walk you through the process of home decorating. Here is a brief summary of each tier of the Home Decorating Success Roadmap.

Discovering Your Decorating Passion *(Chapters 5-9)*

It can be very tempting to jump right into decorating your home and it is great that you have the drive to get started. However, it is important that you spend some time discovering and planning for your decorating project. What separates successful and unsuccessful home decorating is making a plan to turn your vision into a reality.

The bottom step of the roadmap, *Discover*, I think of as the foundation of a house. When building a house you need a good foundation to hold up the rest of the house. Often you can't see the whole foundation after a house is built, so it is easy to forget the importance of it. Without the foundation, the house would eventually collapse. In the Discovering Your Decorating Passion tier you will learn the importance of finding your passion, purpose, starting fresh, and setting goals you can achieve. This action builds a decorating foundation that is strong and easy to build upon.

Creating the Backdrop of a Room *(Chapters 10-14)*

When making over a room I find it is best to start with decorating the walls. I call this the backdrop of a room. You may be starting with a blank canvas or you may have parts of the backdrop already in place when you begin this step. Regardless, a beautiful backdrop will make layering in furniture and home accessories a lot easier.

This second step of the roadmap to successful home decorating, *Decorate*, will walk you through creating a stunning backdrop. During this step you will explore color and create a color scheme. Next you will select a focal point in the room to add interest. You will also discover the keys to hanging window treatments the right way. Lastly, we will put the finishing touches to your backdrop by finding, creating, and hanging wall decor.

Adding Furniture and Furnishings *(Chapters 15-19)*

At this point of the home decorating roadmap you will be over halfway through the transforming of a room. You will be able to see your vision and plans coming to reality. Now in the third step, *Furnish*, is where we will add furniture and furnishings to work with the purpose of the room. There are many mistakes that can happen during these action tasks. Don't worry, I will walk you through each part to help you avoid common mistakes.

You will learn how to select the right furniture for any space in your home. Once you have furniture, I will give you keys to arranging furniture. If you are not planning on buying new furniture that is okay. I will show you how to reuse and repurpose the furniture you already have. Finally, when it comes to home furnishings, I believe being thrifty is key to saving money when decorating. There are many ways to be thrifty and I will show you my favorite ways to get big style with a shoestring budget.

Finishing Touches & a Few Tweaks *(Chapters 20-23)*

The final step in the Home Decorating Success Roadmap is *Style*. In this step we are adding the finishing touches that take your decorating from good to great. Have you ever asked yourself why doesn't my home look like the homes in magazines? Styling your home with home accessories is what makes those homes look stunning. Your home can look like those homes with secret tips I share in these chapters.

You learn the importance of what lighting can do to make your home shine. I will give you keys to styling your home like a pro. It is easier than you think to do. Finally, there are small tweaks you can try if things are not looking complete. At the end of this step you will finally have transformed your home into a beautiful place to share with your family and friends.

Now that you have a better idea of the roadmap you are about to follow, it's time to get started on this journey together. Let's take a closer look at the first step, *discovering your decorating passion.*

CHAPTER FIVE

Step #1 Discover: Discovering Your Decorating Passion

"There is no better high than discovery."
- E. O. Wilson

The first step of the Home Decorating Success Roadmap is called *Discovering Your Decorating Passion.* This step is often missed when decorating, but is very important to create a clear vision for your home.

I understand why this first step is often jumped over. We all, myself included, want to go straight to decorating and making changes. You want to see the results right away. You don't have much time to decorate, so when you have time you want to be spending that time decorating instead of spending time discovering your decorating passion.

When you skip this step, at some point you may find you are running into struggles. I have heard people who skip the discovery stage say one or all the following statements:

- I can't really describe what I want my home to look like.
- When I decorate my home, when I am finished it doesn't seem to work for me and family.
- I want to start decorating, but my home is too cluttered to make a change.
- I make goals to get decorating done, but never achieve my goals.

I know I have said a few of these statements before. There is an easy way to avoid finding yourself in one of those situations. Choose to spend some time in the discovery stage of decorating. You will discover that as a result you have a clearer understand of your wants, needs, likes, dislikes, and what will work for you and your family.

After completing the discover step, here is what you will be saying instead of those above statements.

Statement #1: "I can't really describe what I want my home to look like."

When asking people what style they want their home to look like after decorating, often homeowners are not sure what they are looking for, but they know they want a change. You may think you want your home to be traditional, which is only a start to defining your personal style.

Just saying, "I want a traditional style home," is not enough. Traditional is too general of a term because there are many versions of "traditional." For example, there is Traditional French, Traditional Tuscan, Traditional Spanish, to name a few more specific styles. There are big differences between each of these "traditional" styles. That is why, when decorating your home, you must get very specific and define what I call "*your personal style.*"

After defining your personal style you won't find yourself saying statement #1 any longer. Instead, you will be able to clearly state what your style is and what you like and don't like. For example, if someone asked me what style do I want my home to look like, I would say *Beachy Country Chic*. Then when they ask to describe it I would say Beachy Country Chic is taking a country farmhouse, bringing it to the beach, and decorating with natural colors and tones with furniture and accessories that are rustic or weathered.

Does that give you a good picture of my personal style? I could have simply said country, but that is not enough for a vision. After learning how to define your personal style in the Chapter 6, *Discovering Your Personal Style*, you will be able to be specific like I can be about my style.

Statement #2: "When I decorate my home, when I am finished it doesn't seem to work for me and family."

Believe it or not but each room in your home has a purpose. Some rooms in your home are probably easier to define their purpose than others. For example, the kitchen's purpose is most often to prepare and cook food. However, you may have other rooms in your home that are harder to define or have multiple purposes.

When you are decorating a room in your home, before you get started, it is important to define the room's purpose. How you decorate a room can positively or negatively affect whether that purpose of the room works or doesn't.

Have you ever been in a room where something seems wrong or it doesn't seem to work for the activities that happen in that space? In these spaces, there may be something in the layout of the furniture or other decorating elements that is causing the space to not function in the way you desire. This is why you must define the purpose or purposes of a room before decorating.

In chapter 7, *Discovering the Purpose of a Space*, I will show you how to discover the purpose of a room so you can transform that room to meet your needs. I will also give you examples of how the purpose affects how you decorate. After reading this chapter you will no longer spend all this time decorating a room only for it to not work for you.

Statement #3: "I want to start decorating, but my home is too cluttered to make a change."

Do you have clutter in your home? Do you have a room that has a lot of furniture or home decor everywhere? I have clutter in my home that I am working to organize and get rid of it so I can more effectively decorate the rooms.

I find that sometimes people believe that every wall needs something on it or that having a lot of home accessories makes a room look well designed. Too much decor and furnishings actually has the opposite effect on a room. Over crowding a room with stuff is not good design…it's clutter.

Why do people over decorate? It could be a number of reasons. It may be a fear of having a blank wall or we get too attached to furnishings and we feel we need to use them all. Regardless of why you, and I will include myself in this group, over decorate, in order to decorate successfully you must simplify and purge to give yourself a fresh start.

A fresh start is a clean slate that will allow you to explore and discover new possibilities for a room. With all of the home decor and furnishings that are not serving a purpose removed you can then start decorating and making updates to achieve a fresh design.

In chapter 8, *Simplifying For a Fresh Start*, I will show why purging and simplifying help you decorate more successfully. I will also give you ways to make simplifying your home decor easier by asking yourself a few questions. These questions will help you evaluate what to remove in order to transform a space into an amazing new oasis.

Statement #4: "I make goals to get decorating done, but never achieve my goals."

Do you make goals to work on decorating your home?

Do you find that you are never able to achieve these goals?

Are you frustrated with your progress on transforming your house into a stunning home?

Did you say yes to any of those questions? I have said yes to all of those questions before. Having goals and making a plan to achieve your goals for decorating is an important step. Goals and plans help motivate us and propel us forward on our journey to transforming our home. There is nothing more exciting than finally achieving a goal you have worked so hard on.

However, the opposite effect can happen when making goals and plans. When we fail at reaching our goals it can be depressing and discouraging. I know I have felt this way on a few occasion when I had a big goal I wanted to achieve but fell short.

I want to help us succeed in achieving our goals and plans. I believe one of the mistakes we make when making decorating goals is we make them too big. Because our goals are so big it is easy to fail. I know how important it is to you to decorate your home.

In Chapter 9, I will show you how to make goals and plans that are easier to achieve. Each goal you achieve will motivate you toward your ultimate goal. Whether that is making over your living room or finally picking colors for your master bedroom. You can succeed! Let me show you keys to being successful at planning and goal making.

Over the next few chapters, we will go deeper into the discovery step on the Home Decorating Success Roadmap. It is important to take time in this step because it will create a solid foundation for the next steps of home decorating. When the process of home decorating gets hard or you feel stuck, the discoveries and plans will motivate you continue because now you have greater purpose. Simple actions in this step will lead you to extraordinary results.

Picking a neutral color scheme allows you to accessorizes with any color.

CHAPTER SIX

Discovering Your Personal Style

"I like my house to be unique to me. Sure, I've bought plenty of things out of a catalog, but the way I put them together in my home is special. You might have bought your sofa at a major home decorating store, but the rug you found at the flea market is so unique, it takes your room from 'carbon copy' to 'simply yours' in no time."
-Nate Berkus

Are you unsure about what decorating style you like?

Modern? Contemporary? Traditional? Cottage? Eclectic? Asian? Rustic? Victorian?

With so many options it can be overwhelming to choose what style you want to decorate your home in. However, I believe the answer to that question is none of the above. Those design styles are too general. That is why, when decorating your home, you must get very specific and define, what I call, "your personal style."

Before I discovered my personal style my decorating was haphazard. I would decorate randomly without any style or cohesive theme. The rooms in my home had no connection between each other resulting in a home that felt choppy with no flow.

Once I stopped chasing after every new decorating trend and began focusing on the home decorating that my family loved most, my home decorating vision finally came into focus. After feeling lost in how I wanted to decorate, I now am excited to decorate in a style that truly represents me and all the things I love.

You can find your personal style, too. I will show you how.

What is Personal Style?

Personal style is something that is unique to you. Your personal style is made up of all the home furnishings that are interesting and speak to you. Such as, your favorite sofa that is great for watching movies on, the kitchen hutch that is a family heirloom, and the throw pillows you picked up on clearance at Target. Throw all of these special items into the decorating blender and the results are a one-of-a-kind style.

Yes, you may say your style is more "traditional" in direction, but we all put our own unique signatures on our homes. We are not making carbon copies of what we see in magazines. Instead, when you discover your personal style you create a distinct look that tells a story about you.

People say that what you wear tells a lot about your personality. You may wear the same outfit as your next door neighbor, but *how* you wear it is different because you add your favorite pieces of jewelry, shoes, and purse. The accessories you put on create a new style that is yours and only yours.

Well, the same goes for how you decorate you home. So you may have the same sofa as your neighbor but the throw pillows, lamps, side tables and area rugs you love, make your personal style.

Here is an example, one sofa, styled in two ways based on the accent pillows used.

I find that most people do have a dominate style preference; modern, country, urban, cottage. However, most of us, when decorating or even dreaming about decorating are drawn to more than one style. Often we unwittingly mix together a few different styles of design because we are decorating with things we find beautiful.

There is no decorating rule that says you can only decorate in one style. So mix to your heart's content! If you love traditional and modern home furnishings, mix them. It is far better to decorate with home decor you love than to just copy the design trends. When you try to follow design trends, over time you tend to grow tired of your decor.

Let's Discover Your Personal Style

If you are not sure what you personal style is, that is no problem. I wasn't sure what my personal style was for a long time. The first step to discovering your personal style is finding inspiration. Inspiration for home decorating can come from anywhere, however, here are some good places to start looking for your muse.

- **Flip Through Home Decorating Magazines**: Looking through a home decor magazine is an excellent way to discover the decorating styles you like. I suggest that as you see pictures you like either tear them out or fold the corner of the page.

- **Go Shopping**: Yes, I am tell you it is okay to go the mall and have some fun shopping. Going to home decor stores, such as West Elm, Pottery Barn or HomeGoods, can also help you find inspiration that will lead you to your personal style. Browse the aisles and as you see items you like take pictures of them on your phone. When you are doing this don't think too much about if an item would work in your home, just focus on if you like the style.

- **What Countries Would You Like to Visit**: All countries are different and regions of those countries have different decorating styles. You may want to visit Italy, or at least I would, but Italy is a big country with each region having varying decorating traits. So try to get more specific, such as saying you want to visit the Tuscany Region of Italy or Mikonos in Greece. The style of the cities and country may unlock clues to your style.

- **Take House Tours**: Many large and medium size cities have yearly or biannual Parade of Homes to showcase newly built homes. This is a fun way to see homes of varying home decorating styles. At each house take pictures of decor and furnishings you like.

- **Surf Home Decorating Blogs**: There is a wealth of knowledge on the internet for you to explore. Check out home decor blogs to find inspiration for your personal style. Save posts or print off images that have decor that inspires you and excites your imagination. Be sure to check out my blog, www.DecoratingWithLess.com, because one of the many reasons I began blogging about home decorating was to inspire other homeowners.

- **Check Your Closet**: Fashion often inspires interior design. If you are not sure what colors, patterns or styles you like, take a look in your closet. Take notes of the colors of the clothes you love to wear. Ask yourself, "are my clothes more casual, dressy, tailored, or formal?" Are there patterns you love? (Plaids, herringbone, chevron, etc) What you like in your closet transfers to your decorating.

- **What Type of House Would You Like to Live In**: I would love to live in an old farmhouse in the country. What type of home or apartment would you like to live in? What ever type of house you want to live in think about the style of the that home. Does that home inspire your home decorating now?

- **Art and Photography**: What type of art, sculpture or photography do you love? This can be inspiration for your home decorating style. If you need help thinking about the art you like, you can go to websites that show images of artwork. An easy site to go to is Minted.com. Scroll through the art and see what you like and if there is a style you prefer. For example, if you are drawn to more graphical or abstract art, maybe your personal style is more modern. Save all the images you love.

- **Check Out Houzz**: Have you heard of Houzz? Yes, Houzz not house. Houzz is a great website to search for inspiration and ideas for your home from completed projects by other homeowners, interior designers, architects and builders. Simply put in a search term, such as traditional cottage interiors, and you will find many beautiful pictures of homes to inspire your personal style discovery.

What is in Common?

After you have done a few of the above activities to look for inspiration, it is now time for the next step in discovering your personal style. Take all the things that inspired you and look for common traits. Here are some question you can ask yourself as you study your inspiration.

Do you see common colors and patterns you prefer?

Are the items you like more casual or formal?

Do you see a design style you like more, such as traditional or modern?

Do you see more than one design style you like?

What words describe the images and decor that inspires you?

Write down all things you find in common on a sheet of paper. Be as specific as possible and look for the design style that is dominate.

Now that you have studied your inspiration and have come up with a list of common traits and adjectives to describe the things that inspire you, the next step is to define your style. The formula to discovering your personal style is easy.

Descriptor + Primary Design Style = Your Personal Style

1. The first part of the formula is to pick the best word that described your inspiration. This word could be an adjective (simple), a place or ethnicity (European), or a theme. In my case I picked the word "beachy." If you are having trouble selecting just one word you can use more than one.

2. Next, pick the design style that most closely represents your style. Your options could be: Traditional, Modern, Contemporary, Eclectic, Country, Industrial, etc. In my personal style case the design style is Country because my inspiration comes from many country farm homes.

Follow these 2 steps in the personal style formula to discover your personal style. Here some more example of personal styles:

- Urban Modern Industrial
- Simple Traditional Chic
- Romantic French Provincial
- Cozy Eclectic
- Rustic Modern
- Cape Cod Traditional
- Streamline Modern Minimalistic

Discovering a Clear Vision

The great thing about once you discover your personal style is you will find that you have a clearer vision. Defining your style will guide you in your decorating decisions. If something doesn't fit into your style, you'll know it. Also, if you lack motivation to decorate your home, once you make that awesome discovery of your personal style you are more motivated to get decorating. Nothing is more exciting than designing a room that is made up of everything you love and is most meaningful to you.

My living room before I had a clear vision of my personal style.

One thing to remember is personal style evolves over time. Your preferences and needs will change as your family and life subsequently change. It took me almost 9 years to finally realize that modern design looks great, but it is not for my family. We are more casual country people. If I would have taken the time to do the discovery step, I may have found my style sooner. Over time, as my kids grow up and move out of the house that may change a little bit, but because I was able to discover my personal style I am able to love home decorating and my home.

This room is still a work in progress, but it has come a long way and I am very proud of it.

Now I encourage you to spend some time working to discover your personal style. If you already feel you know your personal style, I still encourage you do this step and find images that represent your style. Remember, the goal is to have a clear vision of the style that represents you and, of course, the most important thing is to have fun.

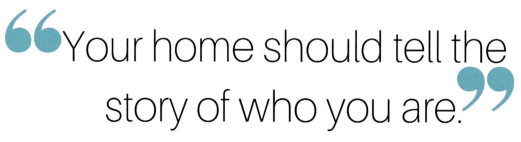

"Your home should tell the story of who you are."

- Nate Berkus

CHAPTER SEVEN

Discovering the True Purpose of a Space

"The whole point of interior design is about creating environments where people can really live their lives and where you can connect with your friends and family."
-Vern Yip

Our Tiny Florida Apartment

Let me tell you a story. Back in 2008 when my wife and I first moved down to Central Florida we live in a very small apartment. We got this apartment for two reasons, it was what we could afford on my income and the location was perfect. The apartment was a 2 minute walk from where I worked and it was right next to a popular shopping area.

The biggest problem with this 600 square foot apartment, other than the flaky paint in the bathroom and the kitchen that was located in a former closet, was many of the rooms did not function very well. I should mention, we rented this apartment without ever seeing the place first. Moving across country to an apartment we never saw was a bit crazy.

Home Decorating Made Simple | 44

Our teeny-tiny kitchen in our first Florida apartment as we started unpacking all our stuff.

There were four rooms in the apartment; a living/dining/kitchen, a bathroom, a small bedroom, and a medium size bedroom. I should also mention we moved all of our stuff from our 2100 square foot house into this New York City size apartment. Stuff was everywhere and there was very little thought about the purpose of each room.

The bigger bedroom became the catchall room with no function and the main room had too many purposes. The only rooms that worked were the flaking paint bathroom and small bedroom; which we decided to make our bedroom. Needless to say living in this apartment wasn't easy. After living there only three months, we moved to a loft-style apartment that was bigger and easier to function in.

The reason I tell you this story is when looking at our first apartment in Florida I believe we failed to take the time to discover the purpose of space. If we had spent some time thinking and defining the best purpose of each space, I believe we could have made this apartment work for us.

For instance, what we should have done is make the medium size bedroom our bedroom. The small bedroom, which you had to walk through to get to the other bedroom, could have function as a dining area. The "all purpose room" as Lynn called it, which had too many purposes before, would function as just a living room and kitchen. Defining the purpose of each space would have made this apartment more livable and we could have save a lot of money staying there.

Why Discovering the Purpose is Important

Our experience in Florida is a perfect example of why discovering the purpose of a space is so important. You may have a similar experience or have a room currently in your home that you don't know what to do with or doesn't function. Rooms that don't function are simply rooms with potential but need a defined purpose.

Discovering the purpose of a space is so important because it helps you create spaces where people can live fully and enjoy your home instead of feeling hindered by the space. Once you know the purpose you know what furnishings need to be and don't need to be in the space.

Think of the purpose of a room as a mission. If a room's purpose is for entertaining then your mission is to decorate and furnish the room so that activity is easy to do. Without a purpose, a room can be difficult to decorate.

Quick Steps to Help You Discovering a Space's Purpose

Discovering a room's purpose may seem hard but all it takes is asking yourself some simple questions. These questions are designed to make you think about the space and move you toward defining the purpose.

1. How do you use or want to use the room? The goal of this question is to write down all the activities you, your family and friends do in the space. Then identify the main activities that happen which will help you discover the purpose of the room.

Try to be as specific as possible. If you say you entertain in the room, write how many people and what you do such as play games, drink wine or discuss specific topics. All of this will help you to create a stunning and functional room.

Here is an example from my home: the den is used by our girls to play with their toys, draw, and read. It is also used by me as an office, which is where I am at now writing this book. My wife also homeschools our 5 year old in the den. In this room there are are 3 activities happening; playing, working and teaching.

2. Write the room's purpose statement. Now that you know the main activities that happen in the space you can write the purpose statement which defines the purpose of the room. Here is the basic formula of a purpose statement:

The Purpose of the (fill in the room name) is to (fill in the main activity or activities).

For our den the purpose statement is:

The purpose of the den is to giving our girls a fun place to play, for the education of our children, and a working space for me.

Hint: A bubble diagram like this one can help to divide the purposes into zones.

The purpose statement defines the main functions that happen in a room. What you do in the space defines the purpose of the room.

I Discovered the Purpose, Now What?

Now that you know the purpose of the room you can use that discovery to help furnish the room. This can be easily done by writing down all the items you need in the room to achieve the purpose.

Again, back in my den, here is a list of furnishings that I need to meet the purpose.

- Storage for toys, homeschool materials, and office supplies.
- Table for drawing.
- Soft seating for reading.
- A table for homeschool activities.
- A desk for office work.
- A place for hanging kids' art and school items.

Now, with this list, you know exactly what pieces of furniture and accessories you need to make the room work for you. No longer will you get done with decorating a room and say, *"When I decorate my home, when I am finished it doesn't seem to work for me and my family."*

I know this may seem like an easy step to skip over but it is important for successful home decorating. I know you probably want to jump right into buying accessories and furniture, that is the fun part. However, all the new furnishings and decor won't matter if they don't serve the purpose of the room. Before you get started decorating, spend time going through these quick steps to help you define the purpose of the room. I promise you, you will find it is easier to decorate.

Beyond discovering purpose for a room, it also important in the Discover Step to find a way to start fresh. In the next chapter I will show you how to simplify and purge to make making over a room more successful.

> "Life is too short to sweat the imperfections in your home. Love your home."

CHAPTER EIGHT

Simplifying For a Fresh Start

"Be as simple as you can be; you will be astonished to see how uncomplicated and happy your life can become."
- Joshua Becker, Becoming Minimalist

Fresh starts are great, aren't they? It feels great to have a clean slate to begin anew without the baggage and clutter of the past. You may feel like you are getting a new start at the beginning of each new year. A chance to make big or small changes in your life to improve an aspect of your life that is bothering you. There is so much potential and clarity in a fresh start each year. I am sure you have given yourself and others fresh starts countless time. But have you ever given you home a fresh start? More on that in a second.

My Story of Simplifying to Start Fresh

At the beginning of 2014, my wife and I had a lot going on. We were expecting our second child, looking forward to moving back into the house that we owned, and we declared bankruptcy. Like I said, we had a lot going on, both good and bad. We took the beginning of 2014 to reflect on where we were in our lives, both individually and as a family. We also thought a lot about our goals, dreams, and where we saw ourselves in the future.

After sharing our thoughts about our lives, we decided we wanted to make a change to lead us in the direction of achieving our goals of living more simply. That lead us to discovering simplicity and started what we call "The Great Purge of 2014." The Great Purge came out of a realization that we had too much stuff. A lot of stuff we had we didn't even use or need.

In the beginning of 2014, we did purging on a grand scale in our house. We probably donated, sold, and trashed over 1000 items. We also were able to pay off some debt in the process. Here is a picture of some of what we purged that year.

After we had gone top to bottom simplifying, getting rid of clutter and purging unwanted and unneeded stuff it felt amazing. We cleared the way for an easier move into our home and a simpler life with less stuff. Purging helped us create a more meaningful home because what we kept were the items that meant the most to us. Simplifying gave us a fresh start to create a new beginning.

Start With Simplifying

You are probably saying, "I am not ready for a Great Purge, Matthew." Let me reassure you, I am not going to tell you to do what we did. We are all or nothing people, and usually when we decide to do something we are all in, especially my wife. Her motto is "Go Big or Go Home." However, what I do recommend is simplifying your decorating. This will help you better plan when you are ready to decorate and start fresh with less distraction in your way.

I know simplifying will probably not be your favorite part of decorating your home; putting the finishes touches on a space is always my favorite. But there is a hidden beauty to a simplified home. Look in any home decorating magazine and you will see great examples of simple decorating. These homes look clean, simple and beautiful. Your home can look beautiful and simple just like those featured homes.

This bedroom is decorated simply and still looks beautiful.

What I love about simplifying and simple decorating is it gives you the perfect amount of furnishing without looking cluttered. I also like how crisp and clean these spaces are with a simple design. There is more focus because there are less items and distractions.

Most importantly to me and you if your decorating budget small, is simple decorating techniques require you to buy less to make your home look beautiful. I believe many people think you need a lot of home accessories and furnishings to make a home stunning. However, less is more when it comes to home decorating successfully and on a budget.

To help you begin simplifying your home and get a fresh start before decorating, here are a few easy places to start.

Simplify Small Appliances on Counters

The kitchen is often the heart of the home and also a great place to focus on creating simplicity in your home decor. A quick way to help give your kitchen a simpler design and appearance is limiting the number of things taking up space on the counters. Things like small appliances, canisters, and utensil holders add clutter to your kitchen. When you are decorating simply you want to remove all clutter.

Slim down the items on the counters by eliminating the small appliances and items you don't use everyday. Have an item or two that adds color to your kitchen, such as a bright colored bowl, tea pot, or hand towels. These items will have a great impact on the simple decor of your new kitchen.

Another benefit to having less on your counters is they will be easier to clean.

Limit your Decor to Only Your Favorite Items

When you are decorating simply you don't have to display everything. Showcase only your favorite items and those with special meaning. By limiting extraneous decor and furnishings, you give more focus on your favorite items.

Simplifying and purging is an opportunity to reevaluate the items you have now. Go through the items in your home and ask yourself if you still like this item? Does it still reflect your style or has your style changed since you bought this decor? This often helps me limit accessories from my space.

Also, simplifying your home accessories does not mean you have to get rid of decor. Instead of getting rid of the edited items, put them in a box and throughout the year rotate items. This way you can change up the look of a room without having to buy new decor...shop from the items you already own first.

My home decor bin that stores accessories that I am not currently using.

Having less decor will also give your home a more designer look that people may think you spent a lot more money to design.

Have you noticed the simple decorating style of many homes featured in home decor magazine? These homes look clean, simple and beautiful. To be honest, I love the simple designs of these homes. Do you?

This is an example of a simplified living room, not a ton of home accessories. The shelves are not packed with stuff, there's not too many accent pillows, and there is no clutter.

If you are in the middle of or thinking about doing some decorating; I think we can learn something from looking at the simple decorating techniques of the homes we see in magazines.

Simplify Your Wall Art

If you love the designer homes you see in the decor magazines another way to simplify a room is cleaning your walls up. Now I am not talking about actually scrubbing the walls...I am suggesting reducing what is on the walls.

Many homes featured in decorating magazine have less on the walls than we do. I think often we believe every wall needs something...that is a big mistake. Simplifying the wall decor to a few items...especially larger pieces or groupings will give a room a simple look that doesn't look bare.

How to judge what size art is good for a wall...well the bigger the wall the bigger the art can be. Generally speaking you want some blank wall space around your wall items (6"-12" is a good range of wall space). We will go over more about wall decor in chapter 14.

Simplify Your Paint Colors

Give your home a simple look by reducing the number of paint colors. In our first house, I must admit I went a little crazy with the color schemes. Nearly each room a had a different color scheme...making the house feel disjointed and far from simple.

If you are shooting to simplify your decor, reducing the paint scheme to 1-3 colors is a good idea. This is especially true when painting the public areas in your home. Limiting the paint colors creates a unified appearance and a great backdrop for other decor and furnishings.

What I suggest doing is have one neutral wall color throughout your home. Then you can layer in other colors with home accessories and furniture. Decorating this way also makes it easier to change out colors throughout the year.

Simplify Clutter

One key to simplicity in the home is reducing things that are distracting, cause stress and aren't necessary. One thing that causes all three of those negatives is… CLUTTER. This is a simple design home's worst enemy.

Clutter is very hard to stay on top of in our busy lives, I know because I am constantly working to reduce and eliminate clutter in my home. Removing all clutter may be an impossible task at first for you, but it is possible.

Simplicity is beautiful in home decor. So if you are like me and desire a simply decorated home, commit yourself to once a week take time to simplify clutter in one area of your home. Purge unwanted items and give things you need to keep a new place to call home. Over time your weekly decluttering efforts will help you get closer to simplicity in design that is free of clutter.

Storage ottomans are a great and easy way to add extra storage and hide some clutter.

Everything Has Purpose in Simple Design

Another thing I notice when flipping through decorating magazines is everything has purpose in simple decorating. This may be the result of reducing the number of items in a room and simplifying clutter.

When you simplify your home decor what is left are elements that are needed in the space to add function and style...which is the purpose of decorating a home.

Look at your home, do your have decor that doesn't serve one of these purposes...function or style? Are there items that conflict with the overall style of the room: if so, remove it because the item doesn't serve the overall style of your home. Do you have furniture in a room that is never used? If so, simplify the furniture to the pieces that are used everyday.

No I didn't leave my toolbox out, this is my wife's papa's toolbox which stores our DVD's.

When you remove items with no purpose in your home you will be on your way to creating a more simplified look. Soon your home will look like the homes featured in magazines.

If You Are Having Trouble Simplifying

I believe the simplifying process is all about looking at your stuff and asking yourself these questions.

- **Is there anything in the room that either you don't like or no longer fits into your personal style?**

- **Are there any pieces of furniture that are not utilized or not needed?** If you have a chair that doesn't get sat in, maybe it is time for it to go. No need to keep furniture that is just taking up space.

- **Are there any home furnishings that are broken or need repairs?** If so, decide if you can repair them in the next month. If you can't fix them yourself, get rid of them.

- **Do you have multiples of the same type of item?** Such as vases, if so, keep your favorite one and donate the rest. Unless you rotate your decor throughout the year there is no need to keep multiples of accessories.

- **If you have something that doesn't work into your design style**, but has sentimental meaning, take a picture of it for memories and donate it so someone else can create memories with it.

- **Do you have too many photos of your family?** I know we all love sharing pictures of our family, and I am not telling you not to but, too much of a good thing can be bad. Limit your family photos to your favorites and try clustering them on one wall creating a family gallery wall.

This is the family gallery wall in my living room.

- **Does anything in the room need to be removed to make the room achieve the purpose?** If so, remove it for a few days and if the function gets better then consider donating or giving away that item. One example is having so much furniture in a room that it makes it hard to move around. Removing a chair or two can make the space easier to use.

- **Is there anything in the space that doesn't get used?** For example, is there a TV in the room that never gets used because everyone in your family watches TV in another room together?

These questions are meant to help you get started with one of the first steps of home decorating. If you answered yes to any or all of the questions above then there is some simplifying you can do. I promise you this will help when decorating your home.

Fresh Starts Are Great

Remember, simplifying is all about getting a fresh start and helping you be successful when decorating. From my personal experience, simplifying has made my home more happy and has uncomplicated aspects of my life.

If you feel overwhelmed when decorating, especially redecorating, then I know you will benefit from simplifying before decorating. Simplifying will give you a clean slate to get started making decorating goals and planning which we will learn about in the next chapter.

Simplicity is still beautiful.

CHAPTER NINE

Making Home Decorating Goals & Plans

"A goal without a plan is just a wish"
- Antoine de Saint-Exupery

Are you feeling overwhelmed by the thought of getting started decorating your home? You probably have a long list of decorating projects you want to work on but feel like you don't know where to start. Your day feels like it flies by between all your activities, responsibilities and taking care of your kids that you are left with very little or no time to have fun decorating your home. You may feel stuck, or think tomorrow you will get to decorating. Yet at the end of every tomorrow you are still in the same place you were yesterday, a month or a year ago.

Feeling overwhelmed and getting no where fast in decorating your home is no fun and can be depressing. I know this because I have felt this way before when trying to get home decorating projects started. I especially felt this way when my wife, daughter Hannah, and I moved back into our home after it being a rental home for 4 years. There was, and still are, tons of project on my to-do list that I want to get done.

When we first moved back in I was getting no where fast when it comes to turning the house back into a home instead of a rental. Between a busy life, baby number two due in a month, and doing our best to stay on budget, I couldn't seem to get anything started, let alone completed. I was getting SO frustrated.

I finally hit my breaking point while staring at the red walls in our entry, which we absolutely hated. Our last tenants painted the entry red, and left it for us change. I decided enough is enough, I am going to start transforming our house into a stunning home that represents our style, not the leftovers from our tenants.

To get started, I wrote everything down I wanted to do. Finally, all the projects and goals that were running around in my head were now on paper. Having everything on paper instead of in my head made me feel less overwhelmed. Now, I could begin planning how I would accomplish my goals over the next few months. For the first time since moving into our home I felt that transforming our home was manageable.

Creating Your Action Plan

This next section will help you discover a way to make goals, plans and to-do lists to help you not feel overwhelmed and to get stuff done. I am here to help you through your decorating to-do list so you can make your house a home.

The first step to creating your Action Plan involves dreaming and writing down your home decorating goals. I encourage you to spend some time, 15 to 30 minutes, write down everything that comes into your mind about goals and dreams for your home. Do your best not to stop writing until you have written for at least 15 minutes. Dreaming is very freeing, so have fun while doing this. I also encourage you ti do to this with your spouse so you can dream together.

Now I want you to organize your goals and dreams into 1 and 5 year goals. This helps you begin to prioritize your goals, which assists when mapping out your Action Plan. Now look at your goals for the next year, pick 2 to 4 goals you want to be in your 90-Day Action Plan. 90 day goals are a lot easier to complete than simply having 1 year goals, because you are more focused on fewer goals.

It is crazy easy to get distracted when decorating your home. With Pinterest, magazines and HGTV, if you have not made a plan you can quickly lose focus and think you need to take on some DIY projects unrelated to your main goals. Sticking to 2 to 4 goals at a time will feel less overwhelming and more achievable.

Creating a 90-Day Action Plan is a key step to becoming more successful when decorating your home. Remember the Discover Step is about setting you up for success. It is easy to want to jump head first into a room makeover, but planning will keep you on track as you move through each step of the *Home Decorating Success Roadmap*. To help you create your 90-Day Action Plan I have created forms to help you list out your dreams and goals. To get the these forms go to www.DecoratingWithLess.com/Bonus.

Mastering Your Home Decorating To-Do List

With your 90-Day Action Plan organized, it is now time to make a to-do list. Your to-do list should include all of the DIY projects you want to do, furnishings you need to buy, and everything else you need to do to complete your 90 day goals. Write these to-do's down on paper. Next is the important step which will help you master your to-do list. Reorganize your to-do list from easiest to hardest to complete. This will be the order you complete these tasks.

For me, these are the benefits when I complete the easy projects first:

1. Quickly finishing some easy tasks gives me motivation to complete the harder tasks.

2. Once all of my easy decorating projects are done, I can then focus all my attention on the longer projects.

3. I avoid being frustrated when nothing is getting done.

Doing the easy to-do's first helps you work up to harder projects, especially if you are new to home decorating. You gain confidence with each project you check off your list. Isn't checking things off your to do list a great feeling? I know I LOVE making check marks.

Now that your decorating to-do list is organized, it is now time to take action and start crossing projects off. Start with the first projects on your list and work your way through that list.

Before you know it you will be quickly checking things off your to-do list. By half way through your list, you may start seeing a transformation in your home. I know I have and I hope you will as well.

Still Can't Find Time

Don't feel like you have to push your way to completing every decorating project. If you try to you may experience some burnout. I recommend a slow and steady approach to finishing your to-do list.

If you are finding it hard to find time to work on a project, that is totally normal, especially when you are balancing work, family and time to rest. I have this difficulty often.

Generally the best way to maintain the momentum on your home project is to do a little bit each day. Even spending 15-minutes a day on a home decorating project will lead to success in accomplishing your list. I will often quickly work on a DIY project before or after dinner for a minute simply to help me feel I am making progress.

Two More Keys To Help

Display your to-do list somewhere in your home where you will see it everyday. This will act as a reminder to work on completing the tasks on the list and motivation to start. The biggest thing to get through your home decorating is to START!

A great quote I heard somewhere is:

"Dream Big, Start Small, But Most of All START!"

This is how many of my home decorating projects start out in the planning phase. Then small step by step I get closer to finishing the project. You can do the same.

CHAPTER TEN

Step #2 Decorate: Creating the Backdrop of the Room

"Home is the backdrop of life."
- Ken Pursley

After spending some time discovering your decorating passion, you are now ready to move into the next step of the Home Decorating Success Roadmap: *Decorate*. In this step you will learn 4 actions to take when starting to design a room. These actions create the backdrop for furniture and accessories to be layered in during steps 3 & 4. The 4 actions of step 2 are *Color, Focus, Windows,* and *Walls*.

The Decorating Puzzle

Home decorating is a little like putting together a puzzle; each layer you add is a piece to the puzzle. As you add more and more layers you begin to see what the final picture will look like when finished. I don't know about you but when I am putting together a puzzle, usually with my daughter Hannah, I always start by finding all the side pieces. Then I put the side pieces together so I have the border of the puzzle. The actions in this step are like the border of a puzzle, they create the framework or, as I refer to it as, the backdrop of all the other layers to fit in.

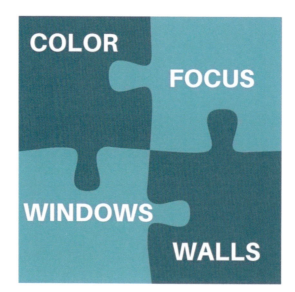

Puzzle Piece 1: Color

Choosing colors for your home can be a difficult thing to do. I get a lot of questions about helping friends and family with coming up with a color scheme. I love helping them because I know how hard this task can be. Often, people are not sure what colors complement each other and will look beautiful in a room. The tricky part about color is everyone sees color differently and lighting can change how a color looks. For example, a paint color will look different when in natural light than fluorescent light.

You may be having trouble selecting a color scheme, let me put you at ease by saying you are not alone. In the first action step of the Decorate process, *Creating a Color Scheme That Works*, I will show you how to make selecting colors for your home easier. We will touch on where to find color inspiration. Then I will help you use a quick step process for creating a color scheme. Lastly, I will show you how to apply your color scheme to the room you are decorating.

Puzzle Piece 2: Focus

When you go into a room your eyes are usually drawn immediately to something in the room. It may be a paint color, a lovely piece of artwork, or a fireplace. This happens unconsciously each time we enter a room. Where our eyes are drawn to in a room are called focal points.

How we decorate a room and with what can create focus. Focal points are important when designing for a few reasons; the biggest is they add interest to a space. A room without a focal point is going to be boring. As you begin to makeover a room, you want to think about where the focus is going to be. If you are not sure how to do this don't worry, I've got you covered.

During the second action of the Decorate phase, *Decorating to Create Interesting Focal Points*, I will show you how choose a focal point in a room. Once you choose a focal point I will give you tips that will help make that focal point shine.

Puzzle Piece 3: Windows

Windows in a room are great for many reasons. They let light into your home. Natural light is my favorite type of light for a room. When you open windows you also let in nice breezes and nature's symphony. The windows are also a great opportunity for you when decorating. They give you the chance to add privacy, color, texture, and pattern with window treatments. All of this adds to the wonderful backdrop you are creating.

Curtains, blinds, or shades are an important part to the overall design of a room. Unfortunately, there are a lot of mistakes people make when adding window treatments to a room. I know I have made mistakes when hanging curtains. However, the good thing is most mistakes made when decorating are easy to fix.

In the third task of the Decorate step, *Adding Style with Window Treatments*, I will show you how to avoid these common mistakes. I will also give you some keys to dressing up your windows to help you be successful when decorating your home.

Puzzle Piece 4: Walls

Do you have blank walls in you home? I will admit I do, however, I am decorating slowly to stay within my budget. Blank walls do give us the potential to add so much interest to a space with wall decor. Wall decor can come in forms such as family photos, artwork, wall signs, floating shelves, wall objects, etc. Adding the right wall decor may have you worried you are going to make a mistake.

In the final piece to the Decorate phase, *Finding, Creating, & Hanging Wall Decor*, I will assist you with this process of decorating those blank walls in your home. I will share my tips and tricks on hanging and how to find, create, and save money on wall decor. When you finish this stage of the process you will be ready to address those blank walls to make a statement in a room.

Putting the Pieces Together

The next 4 chapters are here to help you quickly put the first puzzle pieces of your decorating together. After reading these chapters and doing some decorating you will have a wonderful canvas to layer in furnishings and accessories. You've got all it takes to transform your home and I am here to help guide you along the way. Turn the page so we can have fun and start decorating.

CHAPTER ELEVEN

Creating a Color Scheme that Works

"Color does not add a pleasant quality to design - it reinforces it."
-Pierre Bonnard

One of the first things I do when decorating a room is come up with a color scheme. This can be a fun and easy task, but sometimes it is difficult. There are so many choices when it comes to color. A color scheme is a very helpful tool when decorating a room. Once I have decided on a color scheme, it helps me select furniture and home accessories that work with the colors in my scheme. This is why I choose to start with a color scheme.

How do you feel about selecting colors for your home?

- Do you get overwhelmed quickly?
- Are you scared the colors you pick won't look good together?
- Or, do you find it exciting to go pick paint swatches at the hardware store?
- Do you find it easy to create interesting color combinations?

Regardless of how you feel about color, this chapter will help you gain confidence when selecting a color scheme. I know many people have trouble when it comes to this step. I have assisted many homeowners create a color scheme that works with their existing furniture because they couldn't make a decision. I want to make it easier for you to pick a fabulous color scheme that works and that you love. Picking colors is not as hard as it seems. I will show you the simple process I take when creating a color scheme.

My First Color Scheme Misstep

I remember a time shortly after my wife and I moved into our home, sitting on the kitchen floor trying to pick out colors for each room in the house. When we bought the house we knew we were going to repaint the house from top to bottom. We sat there thumbing through a Benjamin Moore fan deck of paint colors going back and forth about colors for each room.

Back then I thought every room needed a unique color scheme, which is something I would never do today. Most of my color combinations complemented each other. However, I recall one such color scheme that was a big flop. In our kitchen we chose a two-tone color scheme that did not last long. When I finished painting the room, I realized the color mistake I made.

Our kitchen, for about 24 hours, looked like it should be on the campus of the University of Michigan. I would show you the picture, but fortunately I destroyed all evidence of this gaffe in color choice! My wife literally started singing their fight song when she saw it. I do root for U of M on the field, but in my home, not so much.

Luckily for me, it was an easy fix. I switched out the blue color for a different shade and all was mended. It is important to know and be ok with making a mistake from time to time when selecting a color palette. In most cases our decorating mishaps are solvable. Buy a new quart of paint or exchange some accessories to fix what was a disaster for a day. If the mistake is something that can't be repaired right away, no big deal, you will find that most people won't even notice the mistake.

Step 1: Finding Inspiration

It can be difficult to come up with a color palette out of thin air. That is why I like to find inspiration first when creating a color scheme. Luckily, when it comes to getting inspired for color, inspiration is everywhere. Here are my favorite ways to explore for color ideas.

The Color Wheel - You can use The Color Wheel to select colors to form Monochromatic, Complementary, Analogous, or Tertiary Color Schemes. Here is a brief explanation of these color combinations:

- Monochromatic - A color scheme that uses dark, medium and light shades or tones of one color.

- Direct Complementary - Two colors directly across from each other on the color wheel.

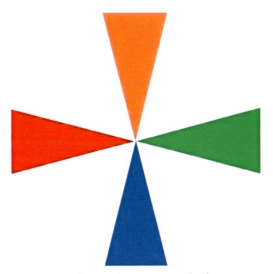

- Split Complementary - A color scheme made by one color on the color wheel and then adding one color on either side of its direct complement.

- Analogous - A color palette of 3 to 6 colors that border or are near each other on the color wheel.

- Triadic & Tetrad - This color scheme is made up of 3 or 4 colors equally spaced from each on the color wheel.

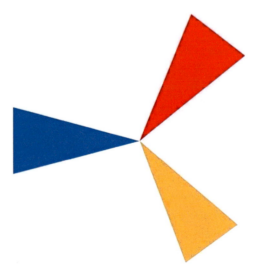

Artwork or Images Online - This is often the method I use when creating color schemes. You can draw color inspiration from your favorite piece of art in your home. I like to look at images of home interiors online and create a color palette from the rooms that inspire me.

I painted this piece of artwork and used it as my inspiration for the color scheme in our living room and dining room.

Nature - Nature is full of color and can inspire a color scheme for your home. Flowers, leaves, and sunsets are full of colors that you can use in your home's interior design.

Home Furnishings & Accessories - If you have furniture and decor currently, these items can help you to select colors for a room makeover. Use pillows, blankets and other home accessories to pull colors from to create your own color palette.

Go to the Hardware Store - You can explore color by heading to your local hardware store that sells paint. Typically these stores will have walls of paint sample chips to choose from. Look at the colors and grab samples of the colors you are drawn to. These colors then can be use in your color scheme.

Color Website and Mobile Apps - There are many websites and mobile apps that can help you discover new colors and manage your favorite colors for your home. Here are my preferred websites and apps for exploring color:

- Design-Seeds.com - This is a fantastic website for color inspiration. On Design Seeds you will discover tons of color palettes inspired by photography.

This is an example of just one of the many color schemes on Design Seeds.

- ColorSnap - Sherwin-Williams - Take a picture on your cellphone and explore the colors in the picture.

- ColorSmart by BEHR™ Mobile - Behr Process Corporation - Very similar to the ColorSnap App, it can explore their library of colors. Simply take a picture and select colors in the picture.

- ColorClix by Olympic® Paint - PPG Architectural Finishes, Inc. - Features are similar to the other apps. Shows you the popularity of each color. It can save your favorite colors in a collection. I like how when you pick colors from a picture the app also brings up other shades of that color. You can also select to see complementary colors that work with the colors you pick.

Fashion - The colors and patterns you see on the runways are often the future colors you will see in home decor. You can also create a color scheme from your favorite outfit in your closet.

These are just a few ways to find inspiration for your color scheme. If you see something that moves you, take or save a picture of it to hold onto when you are creating your next color scheme.

This is a color scheme I created based on this dress using Sherwin William ColorSnap App on my phone. You can do the same by taking a picture of an article of clothing that has colors you love.

Step 2: From Inspiration to Home Color Scheme

Now that you discovered some color inspiration it is now time to form those colors you love into a color scheme. This can be the tricky part for some people. However, I hope to show you how easy this can be.

Color schemes for home decorating are typically made up of 2 to 5 colors. Most color schemes have a main dominant color, followed by a secondary and 1 or 2 accent colors. When I am forming a color scheme I like to use paint chip samples from the hardware store that match the color I am inspired by. This makes it easier to move around potential colors when narrowing down to a final selection.

What are you looking for as you determine a color scheme? You want to create an interesting combination of colors that complement each other. To help me with this I like to use a formula. This formula helps me know what I need to pick to come up with a successful color scheme.

1 Main Color + 1 Secondary Color + (1-2) Accent Colors = A Color Scheme

Main Color - often the main color is a neutral color; beiges, whites, grays, and other earth tones.

Secondary Color - the secondary color is lighter or darker than the your main color.

Accent Color - accent colors are usually non neutral colors; blues, oranges, reds, greens, yellows, and anything in between.

Here are a few examples of color schemes.

If you want more examples of color schemes to help you create your palette, you can download a free bonus called, *14 Fool-Proof Color Schemes That Will Make Selecting Colors Painless and Easy*. To instantly access this free PDF cheat sheet, head on over to http://www.decoratingwithless.com/colorscheme.

Step 3: Applying Your Color Scheme in a Room

Okay, you have selected a color scheme for your room, now what? How do you take these colors and apply it to a room? Taking a grouping of colors from palette to reality can be a little bit confusing.

However, there is a good rule to follow to help you know how much of each color to have in a room. This guideline for applying a color palette like an interior designer is the 60/30/10 Rule.

How To Use the 60/30/10 Rule

Now that you understand main, secondary, and accent color, I can show you how to use the 60/30/10 Rule to help apply these colors perfectly.

This rule states that 60% of the color of a room comes from the main color. Often this is the neutral paint color in a room. For instance, in the room below, the main color is the light tan on the walls. If we could see the whole room, this color would make up 60% of the color palette.

Next, 30% of the color palette is made up of the secondary colors. Your secondary color can be used as a second wall color. I like to do this especially when the secondary color is a lighter or darker neutral of the main. These colors are sometimes used on trim work, such as base and crown molding. It is also widely used as the ceiling color. For instance, in my home, the secondary color is white, and all the trim, ceilings and woodwork are white.

Lastly, accent colors make up 10% of a room's color palette. You can typically use the accent colors as an accent wall and in accessories (decorative items, pillows, and artwork) or furniture upholstery. Just think about this 10% as pops of color in your room. In the living room below, the accent colors are teal and pink. You see these colors are only found in the pillows, accessories and accent furniture.

Applying the 60/30/10 Rule will also help your home look more interesting and appealing. A good color scheme will enhance and accent your home's decor and physical elements.

Missing Something

If you have a room that is missing one of these colors, for instance, an accent color, the room will look incomplete. Accent colors are the frosting on a cake, secondary is the inner filling, and the main color is the cake itself. Without one, the dessert will not taste as good.

The bedroom below, to me, is missing a good accent color. Overall it is a beautiful room, but it is not very interesting to look at because it is lacking a good contrasting accent color.

Saving Money on Paint

I am always looking for ways to save money when decorating. There are so many ways I have found to lower the cost of making over your home. Since much of the color in a room comes in the form of paint, which can be expensive, I want to share some ways to save money on your next painting project.

1. Mix Your Own Paint Colors - Most homes have leftover paint from previous painting projects. As long as the paint is still good you could reuse it. You may not like the colors of the leftover paints you have, however you can create new colors by mixing two or more colors together.

Mixing Rules
- One rule is to mix like finishes. Don't mix eggshell paint with semi-gloss paint. This may result in a weird finish on the wall that is inconsistent.
- Also, when mixing paint color be sure to mix them well so the two colors mix completely.
- Don't mix oil base paints with latex paints.

2. Buy Recycled Paint - You can actually buy recycled paint. Some cities have paint recycling programs where homeowners can bring their leftover paints for the city to dispose of properly or, if it is still good paint, recycle it. Some communities even have paint exchanges where you can get leftover paint for next to nothing. Your choices may be limited but it can save you a lot of money.

3. Ask Family & Friends - If you have family or friends that recently repainted a room in their home, ask them if they have any paint leftovers they want to get rid of. I hate storing leftover paint, so I would be happy to give my leftovers to a friend or family member. This way it gets used and doesn't end up in the trash.

4. Buy Better Tools - Better brushes and rollers can help you save money painting because they apply the paint to the wall more evenly and consistently, without applying too much paint. A good brush makes cutting in a lot easier and faster. Also good rollers help reduce roller marks.

5. Buy Paint in Bulk & Save - Just like buying groceries in bulk, buying paint in bulk will save you money. If you are painting a few rooms in your home, consider using the same color and buying a 5 gallon size container instead of 1 gallon at a time. You can usually buy a 5 gallon container of paint for about $125, which is a saving of between $35 - $50 if you bought the same amount of paint one gallon at a time.

6. Mistinted Paints - The paint store's mistake can be your key to saving big on painting your home. Occasionally your local hardware store will mistint or mix the wrong paint color when making paint colors for other customers. When this happens, instead of tossing the mistinted paint they will sell it at extreme clearance.

I recently bought a gallon of Benjamin Moore Aura paint from Ace Hardware for $10! Wow, right? That is $60 off the regular price. With this paint I have painted my half bath and my foyer, too.

Some stores will have the mistinted paints on the shelves with the other paints and other stores may have them behind the counter. So if you can't find any, don't be afraid to ask a store employee. It could save you big bucks.

7. Buy More Expensive Paint - This tip for saving money on paint may sound opposite of what I should be advising. However, buying more expensive paint can help you save money because in general more expensive paints, for instance premium paint has primer and paint in one, cover better in fewer coats. Which means you need less paint than if you buy cheaper paints that require more coats.

8. Paint Less - Painting less will obviously help you save money. Simply painting one wall in a room can quickly give a room a new look, without buying paint for a whole room. Often all you need to paint one wall is a quart of paint.

The teal accent wall in this office adds a lot without costing a lot of money.

9. Coupons & Discounts - Be on the lookout for special promotions, discounts, mail-in rebates, and coupons on paint. I often see coupons for Sherwin Williams paints in the ads that come in the mail. You can also sign up for Sherwin Williams Paint Perks program and instantly get a coupon for $10 off your next paint purchase.

Check your local paint stores to see if they offer special project discounts. One local paint store in my community offer homeowners discounts for a limited time while they are working on their house. I used this a lot when we first bought our home.

Inexpensive Ways to Add Color Without Painting

Tired of the white or neutral walls in your home but feel stuck because you don't have the money to repaint your whole house. Or do you live in an apartment and you can't paint the walls?

Your budget doesn't have to be a barrier in keeping you from adding color to your home. Here are 10 cheap ways to add color to your home that will quickly and instantly make a difference.

1. **Accent Pillows** - Accent pillows are a great way to add pops of color to any room. Throw pillows also add texture and pattern to a room which are basic design elements. You can purchase accent pillows inexpensively at Homegoods, Wayfair, Target or Amazon.

   If you want to go super inexpensive, check out thrift stores. I recently bought an accent pillow at Goodwill for $1.99 and then recovered it with a t-shirt and it turned out great. Check out my post about *How To Turn a T-Shirt into an Accent Pillow*, www.decoratingwithless.com/tshirt.

2. **Paint Furniture a Color** - Painting a piece of furniture is a great and low-cost way to add color to a room. Pick a color that compliments your existing decor and instantly you can turn a boring piece of furniture into a focal point in a room.

   If you don't want to paint a whole piece of furniture, try painting just the sides of drawers. This is what I did to my daughter's dresser to incorporate all of her favorite colors.

3. **Throw Blankets** - Like accent pillows, throw blankets can add some life and color to a boring room. Plus blankets are great to have on hand to snuggle up

with loved ones for a family movie night.

4. **Artwork & Photography** - A room with neutral walls is the perfect backdrop for artwork or photography. You can inexpensively make your own artwork on a blank canvas from a craft store, check out the *Incredible Piece of Artwork I made for $5*, www.decoratingwithless.com/artwork.

   You can also frame photos of places you have visited to a space to add color and memories. If you don't have any photography to frame read my post on *5 Websites for Free Photography to Decorate Your Home*, www.decoratingwithless.com/Photos.

5. **Flowers & Plants** - There are many benefits of having plants inside your home. Plants improve indoor air quality and can cheaply add color to a room. If you have flowers growing in your yard, cut some and put them in vase on your dining table for a pop of color. If you don't have a green thumb, add air plants or succulents that are hardy and don't need too much care to live.

6. **Lampshades** - Changing up your lampshades is a quick way to add color and pattern. You can inexpensively purchase a new shade at Target for less than buying a whole new lamp.

   If you don't want to buy a new lampshade you can also repaint the lamp itself. For the price of a bottle of spray paint, about $3-$5, you can transform a dated lamp into a trendy accent piece in a space.

I took this $1 garage sale burlap lamp shade and added teal burlap to add some color.

7. **Paint Doors** - Add some color to a boring hallway by painting a door a color. This is a low-cost way to add a unexpected pop of color. If you want to add color and function, paint a door with chalkboard paint. Then you can leave messages for your children. Plus, chalkboard paints now are available in more than just black.

    If painting a whole door in a color scares you, try just painting the side of the door. I did this to my daughter's bedroom door. Whenever the door is open you get to enjoy that subtle accent color.

8. **Table Runners** - I prefer table runners over a full table cloth. However, either can add color quickly to a neutral dining area. You can buy a table runner inexpensively for between $10-$20. You can also make your own table runners with just a few yards of fabric. Table runners are also nice because they are easy to store and change out for different occasions.

9. **Home Accessories** - One of my favorite ways to add color on the cheap is

home accessories. These finishing touches can add so much to a room besides color; personality, style, and memories. I shop for most of my home accessories at thrift stores because the prices fit into my budget.

Before you buy any new home accessories, you may want to see if you have anything you can repurpose into home decor.

10. **Curtains** - Curtains can be expensive, however often if you look around you can find stores that have sales or clearance items. In my family we always check out the clearance area for deals. Curtains are great items to add color to a room because they serve two purposes…style and privacy.

    One tip for adding curtains cheaply is to buy white curtains. They are usually cheaper and can be altered to add color besides more white. For example, you can dye white curtains an accent color or simply paint a color stripe on the fabric.

Easy and Low Commitment

What is great about most of these cheap ways to add color is they are easy to change out and you aren't committing yourself to being stuck with one color forever. If in a few years you grow tired of a color you can again cheaply use these tips to redesign a room on a small budget.

Money doesn't have to be a barrier to adding color to your home. Thinking a little frugally can help you save money and get the home design you want.

Now you are ready to save money and create your own stunning color scheme that will transform your home. Now that you have a color scheme it is time to move on to the next task in the 'Decorate' step. Let's get started.

CHAPTER TWELVE

Decorating to Create Interesting Focal Points

"Be faithful to your own taste because nothing you really like is ever out of style."
-Billy Baldwin

Where do you want people's eyes to be drawn to when they enter your home? Hopefully this will be something amazing, like your stunning fireplace or a large piece of artwork over your living room sofa. Subconsciously our eyes are always drawn immediately to something in each room we enter. The good news is we can control where our house guests look by taking steps to create interesting focal points throughout our home.

What is a Focal Point?

Let's face it, for us decorating types, we always look around a room checking out and looking for cool decorating ideas. The home furnishings, colors, and architectural elements are all things that draw our attention. However, just putting stuff into a room doesn't make it a focal point. Simply put, a focal point in a room is a spot where our eyes are drawn to and stops at. Naturally our minds are programmed to follow patterns and lines. The points where the lines meet there is often a focal point.

Focal points can be good or bad. Hopefully, after reading this chapter, you will only have stunning focal points. Bad focal points could be laundry baskets piling up, which unfortunately in my bedroom is often the case, or anything that would give someone a negative feeling or reaction. Good focal points enhance a room by creating something interesting and pleasing to look at. A boring room can become interesting by adding a focal point, such as artwork. Think of a prison cell; blank walls with nothing to look at but a bed, an industrial sink and toilet. Pretty boring. We don't want our homes to be boring like prison, so we need to add focal points to energize a room.

Creating a Focal Point That Rocks

When creating focal points you first have to choose where you want people to look in a room. Sometimes there is an obvious place where the focal point should be. For instance, a fireplace is an excellent focal point. Other easy focal points could be built-in bookshelves, a coffered ceiling, or large picture windows with an amazing view. If there are architectural elements like these, flaunt your home's assets.

Here is an example of a focal point in a living room; the fireplace.

Now these elements by themselves will be good focal points. However, we want to make focal points that ROCK! For that you will you need to accessorize these features with other decor to make them shine. If you are working with built-in bookshelves you will want to add books and other interesting home accessories to complete the perfect rockin' focal wall.

Not all rooms are blessed with extraordinary features. In this case you may be wondering what to do. The good news is there are many ways we can add interesting focal points in an otherwise boring space. Here are some decorative ways we can create a focal point in a room.

1. Accent Paint - Painting a wall an accent color is a simple way to draw eyes to a focal point in a room. Using accent colors in a room can also enhance an existing focal point. For instance, if you do have a fireplace you could paint the wall the fireplace is on an accent color to really pull eyes in the right direction. Accent paint creates a perfect backdrop for adding wall decor to enhance this focal point.

2. Mirrors - A large mirror on the wall is sure to draw eyes. Mirrors are a great focal point in a small space because the mirror will give the illusion of more space. Good places to hang a mirror for a focal point are over a sofa or fireplace, the wall opposite from entry into the space or across from windows.

3. Collections - Collections, when displayed all together, make a great focal point. In fact the best way to display a collection is all in one place. Breaking up a collection throughout a home is a bad idea because it can look like clutter or it is not as interesting. So, if you have a collection of antique serving platters, pick a wall or a beautiful glass cabinet to display them.

4. Curtains - Large full curtains can make a luxurious focal point. Adding curtains to a large window or wall with a few windows will strengthen the windows and draw eyes to the views outside. In the next chapter I talk more about how to add curtains to a room.

5. Artwork - Artwork, whether one large or multiple smaller pieces together, will make a nice focal point in a room. One key to hanging artwork, which we will talk about more in chapter 14, is scale. If you select a large wall to be your focal point you will want your artwork to match the scale of the wall. Don't put a tiny piece of artwork on a large wall; it won't look right.

I love the artwork above this bed, plus it is an example of using art to make a focal point.

6. Wall Shelves or Bookshelves - If your home doesn't have built-in shelves you can always use floating wall shelves or bookcases to create the same awesome focal point. Simply add some home accessories and books, remembering less is more, to design an excellent focal point in the room.

7. Gallery Wall - Creating gallery walls is very popular in home decorating. A gallery wall is a grouping of items hung on a wall to create an interesting display. Gallery walls can be made up of artwork, family photos, wall decor, signs, wall graphics, and basically anything else you can hang on the wall. They can have a theme or be somewhat random. Either way, a gallery wall is a fun and definitely interesting way to make a focal point in your home.

Here's an example of a simple gallery wall that creates a focal point above this sofa.

Reinforcing Your Focal Point to Rock

Simply by having a fireplace, painting a wall a different color, or hanging interesting artwork does not make a strong focal point. The secret sauce to making a focal point that rocks and will have peoples' eyes drawn to it like mosquitos to a bug zapper takes another step. Everything around the focal point has to reinforce the focal feature in the room.

For instance, if your fireplace is the focal point in the room, to enhance the fireplace as the focal point you can arrange your furniture to look toward that direction. Laying out a room so that the focal point is the focus and can be enjoyed from any point in the room is a secret key to making an incredible focal point.

Blue French Horn Story and The Secret Sauce

My wife and I love the show *How I Met Your Mother*. I'm so sad that the show is over. There is a tear running down my face as I write this. If you haven't watched HIMYM,

I highly recommend it, but you have to start from the beginning. In the very first episode Ted, the main character in the show, steals a blue french horn from a restaurant he was at with Robin, another main character. He does this to impress Robin because she says she needs a french horn over her fireplace. He also does this because he thinks Robin is the future Mrs. Ted Mosby.

Anyway, the blue french horn ends up above Robin's fireplace as the focal point. Ever since then I have always dreamt of having a blue french horn. I don't have one yet but maybe someday. The point of telling this story is to make the point clear that a good focal point can also tell a good story. Whenever Robin sees the french horn she will think of Ted. What do you have in your home that could be a focal point in a room that tells a story about you? That is the secret sauce of making a focal point that rocks. Decorating your home with the things you love is always good design.

> **When decorating my home I am my own worst enemy. I need to stop second guessing myself, and trust my instincts.**

CHAPTER THIRTEEN

Adding Style with Window Treatments

"My decorating and renovation skills are nil - indeed, I once used a shower curtain from Pottery Barn as 'window dressing.'"
- Candace Bushnell

Having windows is a wonderful element in any space. Windows bring natural lighting into our homes and a connection with the outdoors. When you are decorating a room you must make a decision on how to address the windows in your overall decorating concept. In most cases, you probably will want to add some type of window coverings to the windows. If, for nothing else, you will want to do this for privacy.

Window Treatment Options

There are many options when it comes to adding window treatments to your home. Each option has their own advantages and disadvantages. Let me quickly go over some of the more popular options for window treatments so you can decide what is the best fit for your style.

Blinds

Blinds come in many different types and materials. Probably the most common type is the basic vinyl or aluminum mini blind. However, blinds also come in faux and real wood.

- **Pros**
    - Inexpensive; varies depending on material. Real wood blinds will cost more.
    - Offer privacy and adjustable light control.
    - Easy to install.
    - Easy to clean.

- **Cons**
  - Blinds don't add pattern or texture to a room.
  - Aluminum blinds are easy to bend.
  - Less visually appealing.

Shades

Window shades are another option for your windows. I prefer shades over blinds myself because you can add more style with shades over mini blinds.

- **Pros**
  - Available in a variety of colors and patterns.
  - Reasonable cost.
  - Easy to install.
  - Add privacy and style.
  - Good for high traffic areas.
- **Cons**
  - Difficult to clean.
  - When shades are pulled up, some of the view will be obstructed

Shutters

Window shutters add the most value to a home, while still addressing the need for privacy and light control. If you are decorating a more traditional home, shutters will enhance this style.

- **Pros**
  - Visually appealing.
  - Good light control.
  - Simple to clean.
  - Durable.
- **Cons**
  - Most expensive option.
  - Can be limited in color options.

Curtains & Draperies

First of, there is a difference between curtains and draperies. Curtains, which are often use as a general term for all fabric window treatments, are light weight, thin, sheer, and don't block out light. Draperies, are heavier fabric, that will block out light, and do offer more privacy. Curtains or draperies are another widely used window treatment for homes. Fabric window treatments can add a lot to a space and can fit into almost any budget.

- **Pros**
  - Tons of variety of colors, patterns, styles, and textures.
  - Easy to clean.
  - Visually appealing, can fit into any style.
  - Can insulate your home.
  - Budget-Friendly.
  - Easy to make your own.
- **Cons**
  - Harder to install.
  - Need to buy separate hanging hardware.

There are other options for window treatments, however these are the most common. I am going to cover more about curtains because curtains add so much to the style of your home.

Curtains Add A Lot

Adding curtains in a space adds a lot more than simply privacy. None of us want the neighbor to see us walking around getting ready in the morning in our birthday suits. So some type of window coverings are necessary in most spaces. Beyond privacy, curtains are an easy way to control the amount of natural light in a room. If you are like my wonderful wife, you don't want a bright room for your afternoon nap.

Color, pattern and texture from curtains are a great way to add style a room. Curtains can enhance the color scheme of the room. I will often use curtains to add secondary or accent colors from a color scheme. However, if you don't want your curtains to stand out, you can use a color that blends or matches your wall color.

You can choose a solid color or patterned curtains to add color. If you opt to go with patterned curtains, consider your personal style you discovered during chapter 6. There are probably patterns that are associated with your style that could be used in your curtains. For example, if you are going for a Moroccan flair in your living room you could use curtains with an Arabesque pattern. Other popular patterns are stripes, geometrics, and floral patterns. The color and pattern of your curtains will add style to your space.

Draperies and curtains can add texture to a space, which helps create softness and interest. When I am at the fabric store browsing for fabrics, beyond looking at color and patterns, I am always feeling the fabrics' texture. Different textures and fabric types can relate to different styles, too. For instance, for my Beach Country Chic style I could use a burlap fabric to enhance the style and add rough texture to the space. Don't be afraid of adding texture with your curtains.

Think of each part of the Decorate step as adding a new layer to the room. Window coverings are an important layer that add so much to the design of your home. Adding style can easily be accomplished with well chosen curtains.

When you are shopping for anything, it is good to have some knowledge that will help you make a smart decision. When you bought your home, you probably did some research about the home and neighborhood. With the knowledge you found out about the home, you made the decision that the house was right for you. Though not as big of a decision as buying a home, when you are buying curtains there are things to consider to make the right choice.

Here are few tips and questions to help you select the right curtains.

1. How much light control do you what?

If you want some light to pass through the curtains when they are closed, then you want to choose a sheer. Sheer curtains give you privacy, while still allowing natural light to enter your home. On the other hand, if you want no light to come into a room, then the best choice is a blackout curtain, which prevents light from coming in. Blackout curtains are great for bedrooms and can help with heating and cooling costs.

2. Fabric?

The type of fabric your curtains are made of is important, too. Different fabrics will effect the style, mood, and warmth of your room. If you want the room to be more casual choose a lighter blend of fabric, such as cotton, linen, or natural burlap. These fabrics filter light and are less formal. Denser woven fabrics like wool, velvets, and silks have an elegant sophisticated look and give you complete privacy.

3. Hanging Hardware?

When shopping for your curtains you will also have to pick out hanging hardware. There are a few aspects that are important when purchasing curtain rods: size and finish.

Thickness

Size matters when choosing a curtain rod. You will want to choose a thickness and length. Rods vary in thickness from 3/4" to 3". Smaller thicknesses are less expensive, however, depending on the weight of your draperies, 3/4" to 1" rods are sometimes not sturdy enough. Also, the length factors on thickness. For longer curtain lengths you will need to choose rods that are thicker. One more thing to consider is thicker rods add a more formal look while thin rods are more casual.

If you are unsure what thickness to get, my recommendation is to purchase at least a 1-3/8" rod. This thickness has good proposition and will be sturdy for most common curtains.

Length

As far as the length of a curtain rod, here is a good rule to follow: Take the width of your window, including the window trim, and add between 4 to 6 inches to each side. Here is a formula you can use to find out what the length of the curtain rod should be.

Window & Trim Width + (4" or 6" X 2) = Curtain Rod

Here is an example, if your window is 42" wide, plus 6" times 2, means you will need a 54" curtain rod. The important thing is your curtain rod should go past the window on each side, so when the curtains are open they are not blocking the window.

How to Determine Curtain Rod Length

48 Inches Long
+6 Inches | 36 Inches Wide | +6 Inches

FORMULA:
Window & Trim Width + (4" or 6" X 2) = Curtain Rod

36 + (6 X 2) = 48 inches for Curtain Rod Length

Finish

The finish of your hanging hardware depends on personal preference and what fits into your design style. There are a lot of the options for finishes, however, the typical options you will find at most stores are black, white, silver, antique bronze, and various wood finishes.

My personal recommendation on finish is the metal finishes. My favorite finish is satin nickel because it has a clean look. My suggestion if you are unsure on finish is to go back to your inspiration photos and see what curtain rod types are used. Then go to the store and purchase a curtain rod that matches to see if fits into your vision.

4. Choose a Mounting Option

When hanging your curtains you have two main mounting options, trim or wall mount. When you trim mount, you are placing the curtain rod brackets right on the trim. This showcases the actual size of the window. I am not a fan of this option because fixing holes in wood trim can be more difficult. This is why I prefer the second mounting option; wall mount. When you choose to wall mount your curtains, your windows will look fuller and larger. At the end of this chapter I will give you the keys to hanging curtains correctly.

5. Curtain Width & Length

People often make mistakes when buying the right size curtains. They either buy curtains that are too long or not wide enough. You have to think about how the curtains will look when open and closed. Curtains should have fullness when closed and opened. Often I see curtains that only have fullness when open, and then look flat when closed.

I want you to know the key to stunning looking curtains. The key is to get the right width and length to transform the look of your windows from boring to fabulous. Just like you get dressed every morning to look your best, you want to make your windows look their best. Here's the trick: take the width of your window and times the width by 2 or 2-1/2, depending on how much fullness you want. If your curtains are always going to be open and are simply framing the windows then times the width of the window by 1-1/2.

Width of Window x 2 or 2-1/2 = Curtain Width

Here's an example, if your window is 36 inches wide, times 36 by 2-1/2 means your curtains should be 90 inches wide. In this example each curtain panel should be at least 45 inches wide. This easy trick will guarantee ample fullness for your curtains and a beautiful backdrop for your room.

How to Determine Curtain Width

36 Inches Wide

FORMULA:
Window & Trim Width X 2 or 2.5 = Curtain Width

36 X (2) = 72 inch wide curtains

72 Inch Wide Curtains (36 inches each panel)

Now you have the width you need, next you will need to determine the length of your curtains. Your first choice is to determine if you want your curtains to be full, puddling, or sill length. Each length will give your room a different characteristic. Sill length curtains are less formal, while curtains that puddle and puff out on the floor are more luxurious. Full length curtains are great to make a room feel taller.

Measuring for Sill Length

If you are adding curtains to a high traffic area, such as a play room, you may want to do sill length curtains. Last thing you want to happen when your kids are playing is for them to accidentally pull down the curtains. In this case, measure from the top of the curtain rod to where you want the bottom of the curtain panels to be. If you have hanging hardware, such as ring clips, you will subtract their length from your measurement. For sill length curtains you can either measure 1" above the sill or 6" past.

Measuring for Full Length

My personal favorite length is full length curtains. To measure the length, measure from the top of the curtain rod to a 1/2" above the floor and subtract the length of any hanging hardware.

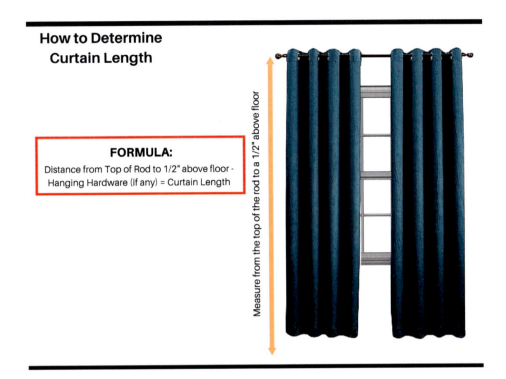

Measuring for Puddling Length

If you want to create a dramatic formal statement, perhaps in a dining room, then a puddling length is a good choice. I also think puddling curtains would look romantic in a master bedroom. To measure for puddling your curtains, measure from the top of the rod again to the floor then add 6" to 9" to that measurement. This will result in ample puddling on the floor.

Hanging Your Curtains the Right Way

Now that you are a savvy curtain shopper, you are ready to hang those amazing curtains you scored a great deal on. However, often when people move to this step they make mistakes. I want to make sure you avoid the common mistakes homeowners make when hanging curtains. The most common mistakes are hanging curtains too narrow and not up high. This typically results in curtains, still covering half the window when open. This is a big home decorating no-no.

To avoid this mistake, it is all about curtain rod placement. Most people mount their curtain rods snug to the window. The right way to mount your curtain rods is high and wide. Mounting your curtains 4" to 6" above the window trim is a good general rule. Then you will want to extend your curtain rod 3" to 6" past the window trim on both sides of the window. When you mount curtain rods this way the fabric should only cover 1" to 2" of the window when the curtains are open. This is the ideal way to hang curtains that showcase your windows and let the most natural light into your home.

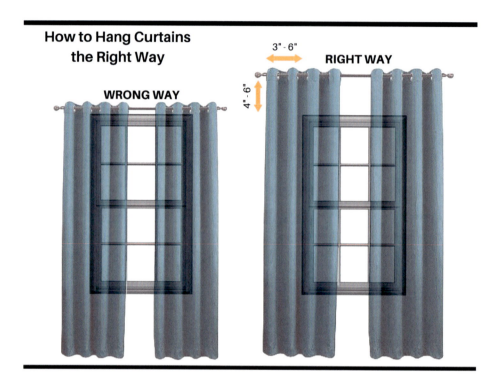

Tips for Saving Money on Window Treatments

Window treatments can be an expensive part of decorating a room. However there are creative ways to help dressing up your windows be less expensive. Here are some of the simple ways you can save money on window treatments for your home.

1. Bed Sheets - If you know how to sew you can use old or new bed sheets to make your own curtains.

2. Drop Cloths - Canvas drop cloths are very durable and can make inexpensive curtains. For $6 you can buy a 4' x 5' drop cloth, which could work perfectly for an average size window. All you would need is two drop cloths to be your two curtain panels plus some curtain ring clips and you've got yourself a set of $12 curtains that are no-sew. If you want to add some color, you can stencil pattern on them or paint stripes right onto the canvas.

3. Buy White Curtain Panels - White curtains are sometimes less expensive than patterned curtains. You can customize your white curtains by sewing on accent fabric, dying them a color that works with your color scheme, or stenciling a pattern.

4. Look For Clearance and Sales - Look for clearance and sales on curtains at the stores, especially at the end of seasons when you can sometime find great deals on curtains.

5. Use Coupons - Using coupons when buying curtains is a great way to save some money. Bed, Bath, and Beyond always sends out 20% off coupons in the mail.

6. Shower Curtains - Shower curtains are often less expensive than curtains. You can use a fabric shower curtain as a curtain, simply buy two of the same shower curtain and use shower curtain rings to attach to the curtain rod.

7. Make Your Own DIY Curtain Hardware - Curtains rods and hardware can be expensive, however there are DIY solutions that can save you money. You can search on Pinterest for some great ideas for DIY curtain rods, such as using galvanized, copper or PVC pipes, wood dowels, and coat hooks.

8. Burlap Curtain - Burlap is an inexpensive fabric that you can make shabby chic curtains out of to accent your home and give you privacy.

9. Make Your DIY Curtains - If you can find a good deal on fabric you can make your curtains. If you can't sew, you can use HeatnBond tape to make easy finished curtain panels.

Window Treatments are your opportunity to infuse some unique style into your home. Curtains are something most rooms need, so why not make them enhance the space by creating a stunning backdrop for accessories and furnishings. Plus now you are a savvy curtain shopper and you know the tricks to hanging curtains the right way. Adding window treatments will be an easy task for you to do, so you can move onto the next layer of adding wall decor.

The metallic ceiling to floor curtains in this living room really add to the elegance of the room.

CHAPTER FOURTEEN

Finding, Creating, & Hanging Wall Decor

"The purpose of art is washing the dust of daily life off our souls."
- Pablo Picasso

Are you living with boring blank walls and it is driving you nuts? You want to fill these walls with something, but you are not sure with what and how to hang wall decor. You may feel intimidated by these blank walls. Is your decorating budget too small to afford wall decor and that is what is keeping you from hanging pictures or artwork?

Is this you? I have felt this way often in my home. Blank walls can feel like they are an eyesore. Since moving back into our home we haven't hung up a lot on our walls. We have a few eyesores I need to hang stuff on. My wife is dying for me to hang up our family gallery wall. I am in the same boat with you. It is now time to stop worrying and start finally decorating those walls to transform your home. Are you ready? Good!

In this final piece of the Decorate step I will assist you with this process of decorating those blank walls in your home. I will share my tips and tricks on hanging and how to find, create, and save money on wall decor. When you finish this stage of the process you will be ready to address those blank walls to make a statement in a room.

Finding Wall Decor

Decorating your home brings life and personality to the space. Wall decor is one way to jump start adding your spirit and personal style while creating interesting items for people to look at. The first task to adding wall decor to your home is to find stuff you love. Have you ever bought something because it is trendy but later decided to you didn't love it? That is why when you are decorating your home it is important you love the decor you put into it. Otherwise you will grow tired of it.

Where are good places to find wall decor to match your personal style? The first thing I would say is start with what you already have. You don't have to always buy something new when decorating. Maybe you have some nice artwork in your basement you forgot you had that will work on one of your blank walls. Shopping from want you have is always the cheapest way to decorate your walls.

If you are looking to start fresh or to want to buy new wall decor I have a few recommendations of good places to shop.

HomeGoods

When HomeGoods finally came to my town it instantly become my new place to shop when looking for home accessories and furniture for my home. I love their selection, which is always changing, and most of their prices. If you are on a budget, this store is for you. It would be really easy to find some great wall decor here, but here are a few tips when shopping at HomeGoods.

1. *If you see something you like buy it*. There are no guarantees it will be there the next time you come. I recommend buying what you like and see if it works when you get home. You can always return it.

2. *Check for quality*. Not everything that is on the shelves in the store is of the same quality. Be sure to check for damage, scratches and imperfections.

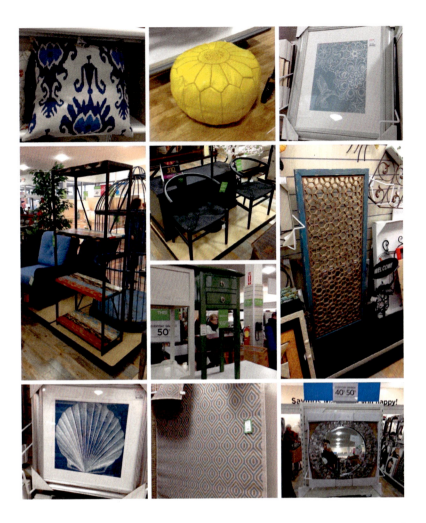

Just a few stunning home decor items that found at HomeGoods.

World Market

If you are looking for a worldly flair for your home's interior check out Cost Plus World Market for bargains. They have a wide variety of items to fit anyone's style, especially the eclectic style. World Market has a great selection of frames, canvas artwork, and other wall decor at good prices.

Michaels

I love shopping at Michaels! Not only is it a great place to shop for DIY projects, but they carry great items for your walls. From frames to decorative letters or wall items. You would be surprised what you can find. Plus, they are always having sales and coupons are always available online or if you sign up for their email alerts. I find the best time to shop at Michaels is at the end of a season or holiday when they mark a lot of stuff on clearance. One more thing I love is they have a custom framing department when you need something framed that is an odd size.

Now if you prefer shopping in your pajamas at home, like I do sometimes, here are a few places I love to shop online.

Etsy

Etsy is a great place to find one-of-a-kind wall decor and furnishings for your home. What I love about shopping at Etsy is that I am helping individuals all around the world support their small businesses.

Another benefit of Etsy is many sellers offer inexpensive customizing of their products. So if yellow doesn't go with your home's decor they can make one in a different color that does. How awesome is that?

Wayfair

Wayfair's slogan is "a zillion things for home" and that is definitely the truth. This is a great place to start when looking for wall decor. Plus you can always find great deals and sales when you shop here. You can easily search their wall decor section to find wall decor to match your style or decorating theme.

Overstock

Overstock.com is where all the other home decor retailers send their surplus inventory and overstock items. Overstock.com then slashes the prices to sell these items fast. You will find everything you are looking for to fill your blank walls at great discounts.

I will say at Overstock there is a ton of stuff, some great and some tacky, so when you shop here you need to do some digging to find treasure. However, they have new stuff everyday to choose from and add to your home's decor.

Minted

If you are looking for artwork or prints by independent artists, Minted is a great place to shop for wall art. They have a large selection of beautiful art you won't see anywhere else. For every piece of art you will know the name of the artist and where they are from. I have even found art from an artist in my home state.

When you find a piece you like you can choose from available sizes, framed or unframed, frame type, and paper quality. One cool things is you can select to have the artist signature on it. Prices range depending on the size and paper quality, but are reasonable.

Low Cost Wall Decor Solutions

If your small decorating budget is keeping you from putting stuff on the walls, I have some tips for you to find or create wall decor for your home. As I said in the beginning of this book, home decorating doesn't have to be expensive. You can create a stunning home for far less than you may believe.

Children's Art

My oldest daughter loves drawing and creating works of art. My wife and I are amazed at her talents and imagination. I think she gets that trait from me. If you have children, you can use their artwork on the walls in your home. Instead of just putting their art on the refrigerator, frame it and display it on the wall.

Some great places to decorate with children's art are in a playroom, kids bedrooms, mudrooms, or hallways. Doing this will make your children feel extra special and help you eliminate a blank wall in your home.

Thrift Stores, Garage Sales, and Flea Markets

I love thrift stores and you should too. Why? Because you never know what you will find when you shop thrifty. Items I am always looking for are frames, artwork, decorative wall decor, and shelving. I have found all of these items and saved myself a lot of money. Now you may have to go to ten garage sales or thrift stores before finding a thrifty treasure, but it will be worth it.

One other key to thrifting success is to think outside the box. Just because something looks one way when you buy it, does mean it has to stay that way. A new coat of spray paint can go a long way from taking an ugly frame into something fabulous.

Family Photos

Framing your family photos is a perfect way to personalize a wall in your home. Creating a family wall of favorite family memories does a lot toward making your home tell a story. Hallways, staircases or other places where people visiting will see the photos are good places to do this.

Free Printables

Printables make adding artwork to the walls in your home easy and inexpensive. Gallery walls can be quickly created by downloading free printables, printing them off and putting them into frames. There is so much great printable artwork you can find out there. In fact, I have a whole Pinterest Board dedicated to Free Printables. Check it out and follow me on Pinterest at www.decoratingwithless.com/printableboard.

Here is a gallery wall I created using printables for my daughter's room. It was so easy and cost almost nothing.

Public Domain Images

I was excited when I started to stumble upon websites where I could download free professional photography and other public domain images to add to my empty walls. Public domain images are photos, graphics, or posters that the photographer or creator has allowed people to download without needing permission. These are royalty-free images that you can do anything with free of charge, which is a great way to add high-quality professional images to your home.

There is some amazing free photography out there that would look stunning in your home. Here are my favorite websites to search for free photography.

- **Unsplash.com** posts 10 new photos every 10 days. You can find some great landscapes on this site. I really like the photos on this website, they are very professional-looking and have great composition. Plus, they just added a search feature which is a big improvement. I always go to Unsplash first when looking for free photography.

- If you are looking for vintage artwork, you should check out **FreeVintagePosters.com**. This a perfect website to find vintage ads, sports, military or movie poster art.

- **Magdeleine.com** posts new photos everyday. Plus, the search feature on this website is very nice. You can search in multiple ways; dominant color, theme or by keyword.

- **TheGraphicsFairy.com** is a resource to find 4000+ free vintage images that can be used for wall decor or other DIY projects. You can also watch project tutorials on The Graphics Fairy to inspire your creativity.

I made this beach theme wall decor from one of the free images on The Graphics Fairy.

- **Pexels.com** is a website to search for free stock images you can use in your home. You can easily search from their 3500+ photos with more being added each day to meet your style or theme.

I created this small gallery wall in my dining room using only free photography and some MDF board.

It's pretty neat what you can create with limited money and free professional photography. I selected several photos from a central theme..*Rustic vintage style.* A grouping of similarly themed photography creates a perfect focal point for any room you can do the same thing in your home for almost nothing.

Creating Your Own Wall Decor

If you still can find anything to put on your walls you can always roll up your sleeves and make your own wall decor. Even if you consider yourself not to be creative, artsy, or a DIY'er, there are easy and inexpensive ways to create your own wall decor. In addition, there are some cool benefits to making something for your empty walls.

1. **Meaningful Home** - By creating your own wall decor your home will become more meaningful. I believe beautiful homes are homes that tell a story about you. What better way to make your home beautiful than making some DIY artwork.

2. **Unique Decor** - You will have artwork that no one else has and can't be bought at the store. Your own one-of-a-kind wall decor. I get tired of seeing the same store bought home accessories. You will avoid having your home looking store furnished by adding your own creations.

3. **Save Some Dough** - Creating your own decor will also save you some money. Money which then can be saved for bigger home decorating projects down the line.

If you are looking for ideas for DIY wall decor projects, my favorite place to search for inspiration and tutorials is Pinterest. You will find amazing projects to fit your budget, skill level, and style. You can check out my Pinterest board, {DIY Wall Decor}, by going to www.decoratingwithless.com/walldecor.

Tools for Hanging Success

Now that you have found or created some amazing wall decor for your home, you are ready to get rid of those blank walls in your home and start hanging. However, before you get started it is always important to make sure you have the right tools. Having the best tools will help make hanging easier and faster. Here are the tools, materials, and supplies you will need.

Hanging Wall Decor Tools List

- Level - To help make everything look straight.
- Hammer
- Cordless Drill - This is a great tool to have for countless DIY projects around the home.
- Ladder or Step Stool
- Pencil
- Measuring Tape
- Stud Finder - This is good to have when hanging heavy items, in these cases it is especially important for your nail or screw to hit a stud to support the weight.
- Nails, Hooks, or Anchors - For most items you are hanging a simple nail will probably do. However be sure whatever you use is rated for the weight of what you are hanging.
- Craft Paper - I use craft paper to test out my picture layout before putting any holes in the wall.
- Printers Tape - For marking where nails go and taping up craft paper.

For a complete list of tools I recommend for DIY home decorating projects, check out my list by going to www.decoratingwithless.com/tools.

Tips for Hanging Wall Decor Like a Pro

When it comes to hanging wall decor, I have seen a lot of mistakes. Many times these mistakes are easily avoidable and can be fixed if you realize you made these mistakes. This book is all about helping you be successful when decorating your own home. I am going to share with you some tips and tricks to making hanging wall decor easy and mistake free.

Tip #1 - Hang at Eye Level

If you have ever been to an art museum you will notice that the artwork is hung around eye level. This is because artwork is most easily viewed at eye level whether you are sitting or standing. Now you maybe saying, "eye level is different for everyone," which is true. For that reason, when you are hanging objects on the wall, here is the guide to follow.

Hang wall decor 57" on the center from the floor.

Here is a graphic to illustrate this rule.

If you are hanging a grouping of pictures on a wall you will want to center the group on 57".

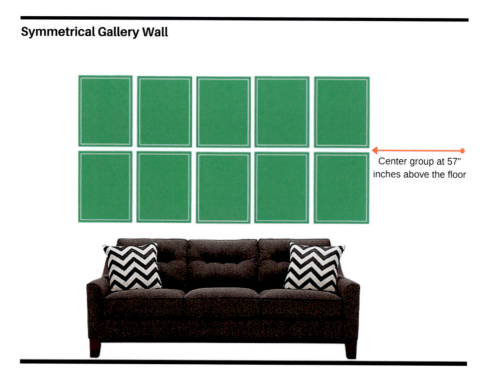

Symmetrical Gallery Wall

Center group at 57" inches above the floor

Of course there are times when this rule can be broken. The one exception is if you are hanging artwork over the fireplace. In that case, hang the piece center between 6"-10" above the fireplace mantle.

Tip #2 - Proportional Artwork

A mistake sometimes made is putting a small piece of artwork on a large wall. When this happens the artwork is out of proportion to the size the wall. So it is important before buying art that you determine the size that works best with the wall space. To do this requires a little math, but it is easy even if you are not good at math like me.

First, measure the width of the wall space in inches. Then multiply the width by .57. So here is the secret formula.

Wall Space Width (in inches) X .57 = Art Width

Let's say you are hanging the art over a sofa. The wall space above the sofa is 72 inches. I multiply 72 by .57, which equals 41. I need a piece of art that is about 41 inches wide for that wall space to look proportional on the wall.

One other side tip related to art size, bigger artwork makes a bolder statement. Also bigger wall art in a small space will make the room feel larger.

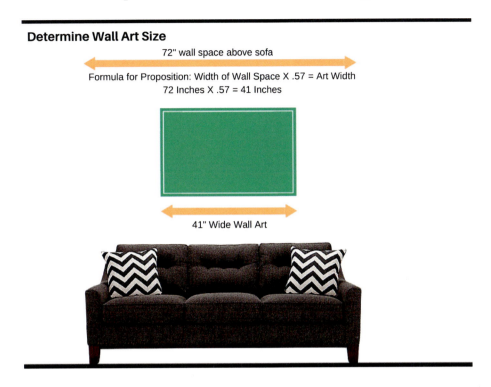

Keys to A Great Gallery Wall

Gallery walls are very popular in home decorating. What is a gallery wall? A gallery wall is an easy and beautiful way to display items on the wall that have great meaning to you and your family. Some items that may be included in a gallery wall are family photos, treasured items, special quotes, or anything that speaks to you and your style.

I love gallery walls. They are fun, interesting to look at, and a great way to express your style or a theme. To help you create a gallery wall here are a few tips.

Mix Styles

Don't be afraid of mixing styles in your gallery wall. Mixing traditional with modern or any other design style will create an interesting wall to look at. I will say, don't mix too many styles, usually mixing two styles on one gallery will work great.

Also, mixing types of items is a key to mastering the gallery wall. I like mixing decorative wall items with art and family photos. This creates a unique look that will look professionally designed.

Stay With A Theme

Staying with a theme or color scheme with help your gallery wall look cohesive. You don't want one piece to out shine the rest. When you look at a gallery wall your eye should look around the whole gallery wall and not be drawn immediately to one spot.

Anchor With Furniture

Your gallery wall shouldn't be floating in space on the wall. Building a gallery wall around a piece of furniture to ground the wall decor is key to creating balance in the space. Great pieces of furniture to ground a wall with are sofas, console tables, and buffets.

Map It Out

Doing some preplanning and laying out of your gallery wall can go a long way to making hanging easier and avoiding too many wrong nail holes. There are two easy ways to map out a gallery wall that I like to use.

1. **Layout on the Ground** - You can layout your art, frames and decorative items on the ground first to play around with the layout. Once you have everything just right get your hammer out and start hanging.

2. **Using Craft Paper** - You can use a roll of craft paper to make paper cut outs of your wall decor. Label each craft paper cut out with the name of the piece it represents. Then start arranging them on the wall with painters tape. You can also mark on the craft paper where the nail should go. This is my favorite way to lay out a gallery wall because you get the best sense of how everything will look on the wall.

Here is an example of using craft paper to pre layout your gallery wall. This makes hanging a breeze.

Layout Idea Starters

If you need help creating interesting gallery wall layouts, here are a few ideas that may help you make a fantastic gallery wall anywhere in your home.

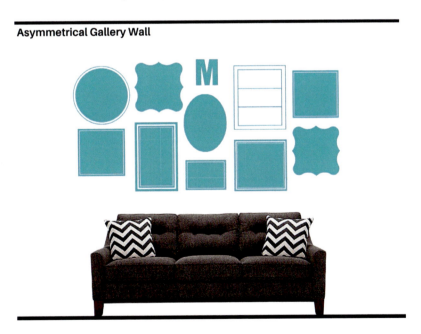

Family

Say Good-Bye to Boring Walls

Are you ready to get rid of the blank walls in your home? I hope you have learned a few helpful tips to make hanging wall decor a lot easier. Now you know places to shop to find the perfect wall art to match your style and will meet your budget. Of course, if you are ready to have a lot of fun, you can search on Pinterest for DIY projects to make your own unique art.

Now you have completed the Decorate step on the Home Decorating Success Roadmap. In the next chapters I will show you how to furnish your home with the right furniture and on a budget. Turn the page to get an introduction to *Step #3 - Furnish*.

This beach themed wall art I created easier and inexpensively with an empty frame, strap wood from a pallet, and star fish.

CHAPTER FIFTEEN

Step #3 Furnish: Adding Furniture & Furnishings

"Furniture is meant to be used and enjoyed."
- Natalie Morales

Now that you are past the half way point on this decorating journey, you should begin seeing the transformation in your home. New color scheme, window treatments and wall decor are in and you like what you are seeing. Finally you are moving toward creating a home you love. Are you ready to take to the next step to decorating success? It is time to layer in furniture and furnishings to make the room a place that can be enjoyed with your family and friends.

Arranging Furniture

Arranging furniture in a room can feel like solving a complex math problem. At times it may even feel impossible to layout a room to meet your needs and fit your furniture. If you are feeling this way, you are not alone. Many people struggle with placing furniture in a room, including me. However, let me assure you arranging your furniture is possible.

In chapter 16, *The 10 Commandments of Arranging Furniture*, I will help you through your struggles with your furniture. Arranging furniture doesn't take a degree in interior design to do. With the tips and advice I share with you in hand, the next time you are furnishing a room it will be much easier.

Adding Furniture

It is easy to simply throw some furniture into a room. However, is the right furniture for you? Does the furniture make it easier to have conversations or read a good book, like this one, or curl-up all cozy to watch a movie? It is important that the furniture you put into a room meets your needs and purpose for the room. That is why you will want select the right furniture.

In chapter 17, *Choosing the Perfect Furniture*, I will show you how to make smart furniture choices. I will give you tips to help you buy the right furniture to meet your needs and style. When you finish this chapter you will be a more savvy furniture shopper.

Repurposing Whatcha Got

You don't always have to buy new furniture when redecorating a home. Sometimes if you simply look around your house you will find you have everything you need to furnish your home. I am a big repurposer. Every time I start a decorating project, I think about about what I can repurpose first before buying something new. I believe my mind has been programed to think this way because my decorating budget is so limited.

You probably have old or outdated furniture in your home that you are thinking you should get rid of. STOP! Before you get rid of a quality piece of furniture think about making it over and repurposing it again. Furniture makeovers are very popular, not only because it can save you money but also because making over furniture is easy and the results can be stunning.

In chapter 18, *Repurposing What Your Already Have to Furnish Your Home*, I will show new ways to use the furniture you already have hiding in your basement or garage. You will also start rethinking the typical uses of furniture, for example a dresser can be repurposed as a TV stand in your family room. Lastly, I will share with you tips for making over furniture to help you be successful.

Thrifting to Save Big

At the beginning of this book I dispelled the myth that decorating has to cost a lot of money. Money should not keep you from furnishing your home. If you are willing to do DIY projects, shop clearance sales, and, my favorite, search for hidden treasures at thrift stores, you can stretch your budget further.

In chapter 19, *Thrifty Ways to Save Money When Decorating*, I will teach you how to save money by becoming a thrifty shopper. There a many tips and tricks to help you decorate on any size budget. I find hunting for deals to be exciting and rewarding especially when you save big. I will share with you my top ways to saving on home furnishings.

You're Almost There

After completing the tasks in the next few chapters you will be almost done with transforming your home. I am thrilled that I am on this journey with you. Decorating a home is a lot of work, but you are nearing the finish line. You are doing awesome. I can't wait to see your results. Please share your before and after pictures on my Facebook page, www.decoratingwithless.com/facebook.

Now let's turn the page and start working on step #3.

Home accessories that have meaning are always the best.

My favorite accessory in this bedroom is the yellow owl night stand.

CHAPTER SIXTEEN

The 10 Commandments of Arranging Furniture

"Decorating is the art of arranging beautiful things comfortably."
- Ruby Ross Wood

I believe I was destined to become an interior designer. Why? Well to tell you why we have to go back to my childhood. As a child and right through adolescence I can remember always changing the layout of my room. About every few months I was moving the furniture around in my room trying to find ways I could use the square footage better. I do this still today in my home. This is the first sign to me that I had a designer in me, trying to express itself by exploring the arrangement of furniture in my bedroom.

I never felt I had the perfect layout in my bedroom, but I think as a result at a young age I realized the way we arrange furniture in a room affects how we are able to use or not use the space. Despite my early exploration into furniture layout, I am still learning how to best arrange furnishings in a room. However, there are some basic furniture arranging commandments that will help you get a good start planning out the furniture in your home.

1. Function Must Come First

When arranging furniture in a room you must start with function. You need to first answer this question how do you use or want to use the space? The answer to this question, helps you know what needs to happen in the space. Then you can make a list of furniture you need so that those activities can happen with ease.

Here is an example; if you use your living room to have conversations with family and friends, you know you need seating for several people. The function of having conversations also helps you arrange the furniture because you will want to layout the furniture for easy talking. So, you may have a loveseat with two side chairs across from the loveseat with a coffee table in the middle. Having the seating facing each other makes having a conversation easy to do because everyone can look at each other when talking.

2. Measure & Make A Plan

Measuring and making a plan of your room before your start arranging furniture is a smart idea. This will help you understand how much space you have. After you sketch a plan on paper, you can explore ways to layout the furniture before physically moving around the furniture over and over again. I have done this for almost every room in my house because it saves me time and helps me discover the best layout of the space.

If you are not sure how to measure a room, I have a PDF guide that walks you through step-by-step on measuring a room in your home. To get this guide head over to, www.decoratingwithless.com/bonus.

Also, if you are not a good sketcher, there are some great programs and apps to help make a plan digitally. Here are a few I recommend:

- *The Make Room* - I recently discovered this online room planner. It is simple to use and you can customize the furniture sizes to match the dimensions of your furniture. Check The Make Room out for yourself by visiting www.decoratingwithless.com/makeroom.

- *Homestyler.com* - This is a neat program that is available for computers or an app for Android and IOS, that allows you to snap a picture of your room, then add furniture to the picture, and new paint colors.

- *RoomSketcher.com* - Is another free online room planner, which also creates 3D views of your plan. You can start from predetermined room shapes and then customize to your specific dimensions. You can also start from scratch.

3. Create Zones

When you are laying out furniture it is good to create zones, especially in big or long rooms and rooms with multiple functions. Creating zones helps break up the room into different purposes. For example, in my family room, which is a long and skinny room, we have two zones. One zone a lounging area facing the fireplace and the second smaller zone on the other end of the room is for reading.

For small spaces, creating zones is very important because often rooms have to do double and triple duty. In this case, planning is key and requires thinking more outside the box.

4. Find Balance

An important element of interior design is balance. When it comes to home decorating balance refers to the distribution of visual weight in the room. The furniture and architectural elements (like a fireplace or windows) in a space all create visual weight in your room.

We want our rooms to be balanced and not lop-sided like a sinking ship. To create a balanced room, avoid placing all your furniture on one side of a room. If you place a sofa on one side of the room, across from the sofa you will want to place something of equal visual weight to balance the room. That could be a bookcase, windows, a fireplace, two side chairs, etc. The easiest way to create balance is with a symmetrical furniture layout. Here is an example of symmetrical furniture arrangement.

See next page for a diagram showing the difference between a balanced and unbalanced furniture layout.

5. Let Your Furniture Breathe

When at all possible, arrange your furniture off the walls to create a more interesting space. When furniture is arranged against the walls it actually makes the room feel smaller. In some rooms this is unavoidable due to space limitations. However, even a few inches from the walls can make a big difference.

A nice way to get your loveseat or sofa off the wall is by putting a console table behind the piece of furniture. This allows the sofa to sit off from the wall, plus you can style the console table with lamps and other home accessories.

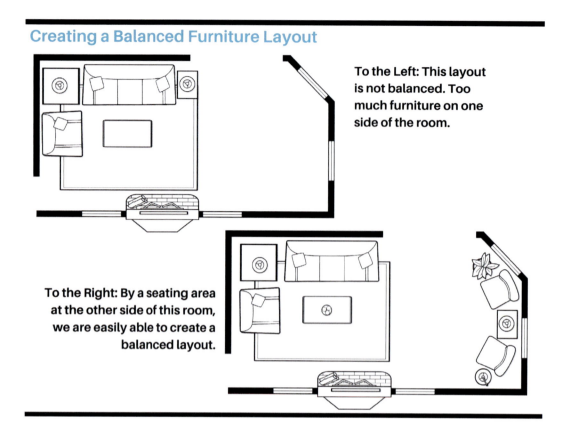

6. Don't Forget Room for Circulation

Remember, in any given room people have to be able to move about without tripping over furniture or each other. When arranging furniture, think about how people will travel through and throughout the space. Sometimes I will draw the travel pattern on my floor plan so I know where not place furniture.

To help you know how much room you need for circulation here are some key furniture clearance dimensions.

- 15" - 18" between a sofa and a coffee table.

- 7' between the sofa and a TV, this can vary depending on the size of your TV. The larger the TV screen the greater difference from the TV to your seating should be.

- Minimum 36" between furniture and a wall.

- 36" around dining chairs.

- 24" between dining chairs to avoid knocking elbows.

- 3' or 6' between seating furniture and 10' between between seating options that are across from each other to help conversation and with crowding.

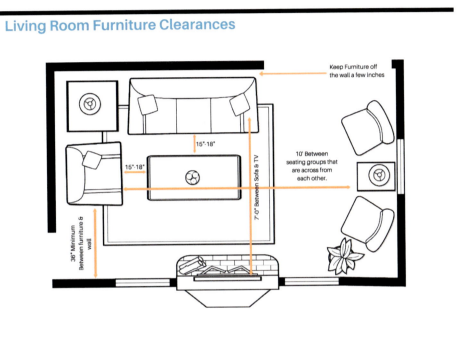

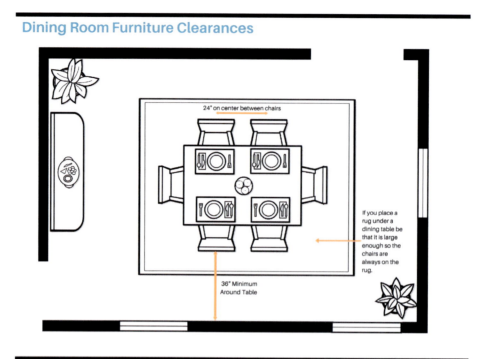

7. Anchor Area Rugs

Area rugs add a lot of style and softness to a room. Rugs are also a wonderful way to to define different zones in a room. However, often people make the common mistake of putting the wrong size area rug in a room. One of the problems with an undersized rug is it makes a room feel smaller. A tiny rug in a large room just looks silly, which is the last thing you want people to think when they enter your home.

How do you determine the right size rug for your room?

Sizing an area rug for your furniture layout is easier than you may think. The goal is that the rug should be anchored by your furniture. This means your furniture needs to be sitting on the rug and not off of it. Now the whole furniture doesn't have to be on the rug, but 6" - 12" of the rug should be under the furniture.

Right & Wrong Way to Place a Rug

To the Left: This is the wrong to place a rug. This rug is too small.

To the Right: This is the correct way to place a rug. The rug is anchored by the furniture because 6"-12" of under is under the sofa and chair.

6"-12" under furniture

For a rug in a dining room, the rug size should be 36" larger than the table on all sides. This way the chairs are always on the rug even when pulled out. Nothing is worse than sitting on a dining chair that is half on and half off a rug.

Common rug sizes you will find are 5x8, 6x9, 8x10, 9x12, 10x14, and 12x15. Measure the width and depth of your furniture arrangement first. Then pick the size which best fits your furniture layout.

8. Orient Furniture Toward the Focal Point

Back in chapter 12, you learned about the importance of focal points and how to choose a focal point for your room. Once you have your focal point it helps you to arrange the furniture in the room. Start by facing the largest piece toward the main focal point in the room. This anchors the layout and focal point. Then play with layering in the other side furniture in the room. Ideally, wherever you sit in the room you are able to enjoy your focal point.

9. Avoid Angles

Unless the room you are arranging furniture in has angles, avoid putting your furniture on an angle. Putting your furniture on an angle is not the most efficient way to use space. Angled furniture in a square or rectangle room will waste space and create areas of the room that are dead zones. Angles also act as barrier in a room, dividing the space in a non functional way.

10. Light the Whole Space

In chapter 21, *Highlighting & Accenting a Space With Lighting*, we will be talking in more depth about lighting a room properly. However, when arranging furniture in a room it is important to start thinking about lighting the room. It is important that you light the whole space to avoid having a dark spot in the room. This can be achieved by adding table and floor lamps in addition to overhead and natural light. Lamps also are great way to add color and style in a room.

Basic Steps When Arranging Furniture

1. Measure your room and furniture.

2. Make a plan on graphic paper or with an app so you can play with your layout.

3. Determine how you use the space in real-life.

4. See if you can repurpose the furniture you have or if you need to purchase some new pieces.

5. Decide if you need to create zones to break up the room.

6. Start with your focal point and orient furniture around the focal point.

7. Think about traffic flow and clearances between furniture in the space.

8. Place a rug under the furniture layout that is the right size to define the space.

9. Add lighting throughout the space.

10. Tweak the layout until it feels right. You will know when it is just right. Don't worry if it takes a few tweaks to make it right.

Follow these steps and commandments to help you arrange furniture throughout your home. Remember that your furniture layout can change, so if you are unsure about a layout, test it out for a week to see if it works. Then change it if necessary.

Remember that the ultimate goal of your furniture is to help you achieve the function of the space. If that is happening then you have done it right. Now, let's talk about choosing the right furniture for your home.

> "Decorating a home is more like a marathon than a sprint. Enjoy the journey."

The furniture in this living room is nicely arranged for conversation and watching a movie.

CHAPTER SEVENTEEN

Choosing the Perfect Furniture

"I look at every piece of furniture and every object as an individual sculpture."
- Kelly Wearstler

Back when my wife and I were dating we both moved into new apartments. I moved into a teeny tiny studio apartment and she moved into a one bedroom apartment around the corner from my place. Living in these apartments was the first time for both of us to live without roommates. For Lynn, this meant she needed to get some new furniture.

At this point I was attending interior design school, so I was excited to help her shop for furniture. We ended up at Art Van Furniture to find new living room furniture. We walked around the showroom looking at all the perfectly arranged and decorated vignettes. Of course, Lynn's budget for a new sofa and side chair wasn't huge, so we drooled over more expensive furniture for a while until we came across a marked down leather living room set.

The living room set was your classic traditional overstuffed sofa and side chair. It was super comfy, great for naps, and room to spoon. Lynn decided this was the perfect furniture for her new apartment. She also got a nice coffee table with drawer storage and a large area rug. This was everything she needed to furnish her new place.

Fast forward ten years and we still have that furniture set in our living room! This furniture has gone through a lot; more moves than you can count on one hand, dogs, cats, spills and children have all left their mark on this furniture. Now I must admit, I hate the size of this furniture. It is so huge and takes up so much space in a room, it annoys the interior designer in me. I would much rather have a smaller scale comfy loveseat with side accent chairs. It is so hard to arrange a room with this Titanic size furniture. I have cursed this sofa a few times as I have moved it around trying to figure out the best layout.

Nonetheless, we have made this furniture work for us for over ten years. I am sure the furniture will eventually be replace with something new. But for now, it works for us and as a designer I do my best to make this tan tank look stunning. I guess it is the perfect furniture for us.

This sofa must be built like a tank for all its been through. It is super comfy which is wonderful for lazy afternoons.

To Find the Perfect Furniture, Start with Purpose

I may be starting to sound like a broken record now when it comes to purpose. But before you think about the color and style of your furniture you need to think about the purpose and function of the room. I know it is easy to get caught up in colors and gorgeous fabric patterns. I love looking at fabrics first, too. But if your goal is to find the right furniture for a space, then go back to how you plan to use the space.

Answer these questions to help you determine what furniture is right for the room.

- *What is this room primarily going to be used for?* (Ex. Watching television)

- *How many people will be in this room at one time?* (Ex. No more than 6)

- *Is this a formal or more causal room?* (Ex. Always a causal place to hangout with family and friends)

- *What activities will happen in this room?* (Ex. Play boardgames, watching sports, & reading in the evening)

- *What do I need in the room to make the primary purpose easy to do?* (Ex. Entertainment center, a sofa and side chairs for 6 people, and table to play board games on)

The goal of these questions is to help you drill down on how the room is used. From this you can make a list of furniture you will need. Only put furniture on the list that will serve the purpose of the room. If you have a piece of furniture that doesn't fit the purpose…GET RID OF IT! Well, you don't need to really get rid of it. However, move it to another room where it can be useful.

10 Tips to Selecting Perfect Furniture

1. The Type of Wood Makes a Difference

If you are looking for furniture that will last, know your woods. When it comes to furniture go with quality over quantity. For quality furniture you will want to pay attention to the type of wood used to construct it. Solid wood furniture is the most sturdy and will last a lifetime with good care. Veneer furniture is constructed with a substrate, often a plywood, with a thin layer of a more expensive wood. Veneer furniture is durable and less expensive than solid wood. Lastly, you have furniture made from particleboard with a laminate top layer. Particleboard is the least expensive, but sacrifices on durability.

2. Lookout For Glue & Nails

Buying furniture is a big investment. When you buy a car you do more than just look before buying. You test drive it, look under the hood, and do a close examination for bumps, rust and scratches. You should do the same thing for furniture to avoid buying a lemon.

When doing a close examination, look for how the wood pieces are joined. Avoid joints that are simply glues or nailed together. This construction is much weaker than all wood joinery. With wood joinery the wood pieces hook together resulting in, strong construction that will be less prone to fail.

Here are some common wood joinery types from www.britannica.com.

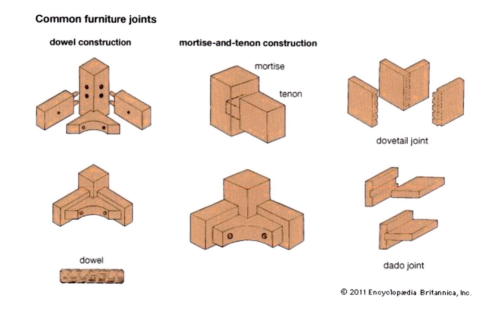

3. Slam the Drawers & Doors

Now don't literally slam the drawers and doors. In my house that will get you put into time out. However, you do want to test the drawers to make sure they open fully and close easily. Also, make sure the latches work and the doors close evenly. Lastly, be sure to examine the pulls and knobs for looseness.

4. Look at the Legs

Quality furniture will have securely fastened legs. Legs should be screwed into the base of the furniture frame. If you are purchasing a sofa, look for the fifth leg in the center. Move around the furniture to see if the legs bow, bend, or wobble.

5. Your Lifestyle & Upholstery

Think about your lifestyle and what type of upholstery would work best for you. For instance, I have two kids that have a tendency to spill and drop food on the sofa and use the furniture as a trampoline. Our family room furniture has faux leather instead of fabric. This material is easy clean and doesn't stain as easily as fabric upholstery.

Think about what type of upholstery works for you and your family. Also, don't rule out furniture with slipcovers. Now I am not talking about the slipcover you can buy at the store, but furniture that comes with a slipcover that was custom made for that piece of furniture. This type of furniture looks great and is easy to clean when life's messes happen.

Furniture is made to be used and sat on. Don't buy furniture that you are going to not want people to sit on because you are too worried something may get ruined. Life is too short to stress over a spill. I have so many stories about homes having furniture that no one is allowed to sit on. That is so silly, unless you have some historical piece of furniture that George Washington once sat in, furniture is meant to be used.

6. Have One Statement Piece

Adding a statement piece of furniture is a good idea to add personality and interest to a room. Now you don't need to go crazy. A simple way to add a unique piece is having an accent chair that is different from the rest of the furniture. This chair could be different in style, color, pattern, or texture. The nice thing about a statement piece is they are unexpected. If you are sheepish about making a bold statement try something that is not so bold. A simple change in fabric pattern will do the trick.

This is the statement piece in my living room. I was a vintage stereo cabinet that I made over to become a sofa table. The color stands out against the rest of the furniture in the room.

7. Don't Be Afraid of Mixing Styles

Emily from DecorChick.com, once told me her "…favorite tip would be to not be afraid to mix different styles. If you like some traditional elements, and some modern, combine them in a way where it will work in your home. It will add more interest and tell more of a story about you and your home."

Variety is the spice of life. Don't worry that you are making a mistake by mixing it up. Decorate your space by mixing and matching furnishings from different styles. If you have furniture that doesn't match in style but that you love, use that to your advantage when furnishing the room. Put you favorite furniture together to create an interesting and eclectic mix of style. By doing this your home will look unique, personalized and interesting.

If you are buying new furniture I recommend buying one piece of furniture at a time. Not only does this spread out the furnishing costs, which is always nice, it also will allow you find dynamic and interesting furniture to mix together.

8. Color, Pattern, & Texture

You can add style to your furnishings by adding color, pattern and texture. There are many ways you can accent your furniture with colors, patterns, and textures. However, the two ways I like to add these elements into my furniture are with an accent chair and pillows.

Accent chairs are a good way to add color and pattern with furniture. With the major pieces of furniture stick with neutral colors; beige, grays, tans, browns or black. Then accessorize with throw pillows to layer in accent colors, patterns and textures.

9. Measure Before You Buy

Before buying new furniture, be sure to measure it. Make sure the piece will fit the room. This is why is it smart to measure the room and make a plan. Also, think about how the furniture will get into your house. Make sure it isn't too big fit through doors, stairs and hallways.

We had a 4-post queen bed frame that we bought for the house we rented. The bed frame fit into the rental house perfectly, but when we moved into our home it couldn't fit up the stairs. This was a huge bummer. We ended up begrudgingly selling that bed frame and got a new frame that would fit up our tricky stairs.

10. Cushion & Spring Test

When buying furniture, be sure to check the cushion and springs. Sit on the sofa or chair to check the firmness. Is the cushion comfortable for you? Is the seat too soft? Is it difficult to get out of the chair? These are questions to consider when sitting in the furniture before buying.

If you really like a piece of furniture at a store, but the cushion is not comfortable, check to see if there are cushion options. Sometimes furniture stores can order the same sofa with different cushions to match the degree of firmness you are looking.

Furniture Tips For Small Spaces

Many of us have small rooms that we wish were bigger. Without knocking down walls there are a few ways the furniture you select can make a small space feel bigger. If you have a small room, here are a few tips to consider.

Furniture with Exposed Legs

Furniture with exposed legs will help make a room look bigger. This is one of those psychological ways to make a room bigger. When our eyes can see under, through or past furniture a small space appears larger. A big overstuffed sofa with a skirt hiding the legs interrupts our vision. This results in a room looking smaller, not good in a small room. In your small space, opt for furniture that is lighter in scale with visible legs that are slender. Also, furniture with glass tops or lucite is also a big plus.

Less Is More

In your small room...LESS IS MORE. Over decorating is one of the common mistakes we make when dealing with a small room. Too much in a small room will only enhance the fact that the room is small.

Eliminate any furnishings that are not essential. Keep wall decor and furniture to a minimum. Instead of having a sofa and side chair...just have a sofa or love seat. Reducing the furnishings may seem wrong, but it will work. Too much in a small room draws the wall in visually. Small rooms with less furniture and decor feel open, inviting and...yes... BIGGER.

Double Duty

In a small room you want to maximize the space, however, once again, less is more. What do you do to maximize the space without adding too much or creating clutter? Add furniture that works double duty.

Ottomans and coffee tables with storage are a great idea. Media consoles that hide the equipment and movies. Anything that serves more than one purpose is good for a small room. So limit single use items and go for multipurpose furnishings. This will help you eliminate stuff, cut clutter and make a small space bigger.

Tips For Saving Money on New Furniture

So what do you do when your budget is limited and you need new furniture? Here is a practical guide on how to save money on furniture for your home.

1. Shop Clearances & Sales

Many furniture stores have clearance centers or areas in their store. These are the areas to shop in if you are looking for budget friendly furniture. Your selections may be reduced from the rest of the store but the good news for your purse is the prices are often cut in half.

If you are looking for the good sales, Memorial Day and Veterans Day are great, but the best sales are during 4th of July and even Christmas.

2. Buy with Cash

Take the Dave Ramsey approach and paid for your next furniture purchase with cash and not credit. Paying with cash can give you a chance to negotiate a better price. Start fanning out the Benjamins in front of the sales associates and see what kind of bargains you get.

Your strategy could be to come in with a hundred dollars less than the cost of the furniture you are looking to buy. Then put all your cards on the table and say this is all have to spend or I have to go elsewhere. The key is to be ready to walk away if they say no.

Now I wouldn't try this method at any chain furniture stores. They probably won't reduce their prices or bargain with you. Good stores to try this at are locally owned stores or consignment shops. These stores are usually more open to offers.

3. Slipcover It

If you are tired of the upholstery on your living room sofa and want to save money on new furniture, instead of purchasing a new sofa buy a slipcover. I know you may be thinking slipcovers are ugly, they don't fit right, and never look good. I would say think again. Slipcovers have come a long way since your parents' days.

4. Post on Facebook

When looking for a deal on living room furniture, post an "in search of" (ISO for short) status on Facebook. Do not be surprised if in a few minutes after posting you have comments with people offering to give or sell you some unwanted furniture. You can post on your timeline or, like I do probably at least once a month, on an Online Garage Sale Facebook group. This is exactly how I got my $45 queen bed frame and $50 freezer chest. You can also do this on Craiglist, but I perfer Facebook because it feels safer to me.

5. Garage Sales

Going to garage sales is a frugal shopper's idea of a good time. My wife and I love spending a Saturday morning going around to garage sales.

I am always on the lookout for good deals on furniture and home decor. Lynn is always looking for clothes for our girls. When in need for low cost furniture garage sales are the perfect place to start looking. When you are shopping garage sale furniture look for a quality piece.

If you are looking a for a sofa, be sure to sit on it to test the cushion and springs. If you sink into it then the springs are probably in bad shape. Also, lift up the cushions and give the upholstery an inspection for damage. Do not hesitate to offer less than the tag price to get a better deal. Ask if they would accept a lower price and point out any flaws to show them why your offer is reasonable.

6. Drive Around

I will admit, I have curbside furniture in my home. I have a night stand, a sofa, an office chair and a bench that were all sitting on the curb while I was driving by. If you were in the car with me, you would probably notice me scanning the curbs for furniture and furnishings. The fact is, people throw out a lot of nice furniture that just needs a little TLC.

If you have zero funds in your budget for furniture then drive around on garbage days to find some furniture treasure. As I say, "One person's trash is the perfect furniture piece for my home." It doesn't get more affordable than free.

This is just a few of the curbside treasure I have found around town.

What I Don't Recommend When Buying Furniture

When you have a limited budget it is easy to be tempted to use credit cards or financing offers.

No interest offers and high credit limits are very dangerous if you have limited income. It can be easy to fall into the trap of credit cards to purchase furniture.

I have used credit cards and financing to buy new furniture and in the end this method has caused me financial issues later. It is because of credit cards and other financial mistakes that my furniture budget is so limited.

So, from my personal experience, these are not the best avenues to buy home furnishings for your home. You commit yourself to credit card payments that you can never guarantee you will be able to pay in the future. You never know when you or your spouse may lose their job, which could cause the low furniture payment to be a big burden on your family.

Cash is the Way to Go

The way I always recommend to buy anything for your house is… CASH.

That way you are less likely to spend too much.

If you are buying new furniture I hope you feel better prepared now. It is important to be a smart shopper when looking for the perfect furniture. It can be easy to make a wrong choice, but now you have some tips to help guide you to a smart buy. I encourage you to look back at the advice in this chapter anytime you are looking for furniture.

If you are not looking for furniture, in the next chapter you will find out ways to repurpose the furniture you already have.

CHAPTER EIGHTEEN

Repurposing the Furniture Your Already Have

"Decorators should never insist on throwing out everything the client has. Even when they are far from perfect, loved possessions add personality."
- Billy Baldwin

You probably have seen on Pinterest the many ways people have repurposed furniture for their home. Have you tried repurposing any old furniture? If so, you know how rewarding it is to repurpose an ugly old piece of furniture into a centerpiece of a room. If you haven't tried your hands at repurposing something, that's okay. I will get you to the point where you are confident enough to try a furniture makeover. I will show you a few simple ways to transform furniture you may have in your basement or attic.

Why is Repurposing So Awesome?

There are many reasons why repurposing is so awesome and popular. I am sure you have seen many furniture makeovers. It is pretty cool to see how a DIY'er can transform an old piece of furniture into a beautiful and unique piece. Also, have you seen how people take a common item and reinvent it into an amazing new use?

One of the reason I think repurposing is so great is saving quality furniture and useful items from ending up in the landfill.

According to the U.S. EPA, in 2009, 9.8 million tons of furniture ended up in the landfills.

This is so sad because I am sure many good piece of furniture ended up there. I have saved many items, much to my wife's dismay at times, that were destined for the landfill. Most of this furniture simply needed a little TLC.

I also love transforming furniture because I save money furnishing my home and you can, too. Most of the furniture I have restored cost me nothing or only a few dollars.

People are happy to give you furniture that they think is old and in the way. To make these pieces of furniture beautiful again often just requires a coat of paint. Which won't cost you much. Far less than buying new furniture.

It addition, repurposing gives you the opportunity to create something that is unique and perfect for your home. All it takes is a little thinking outside the box and looking past the current ugliness of a piece of furniture. It is so worth it.

Simple Ways to Repurpose Furniture You Have

It doesn't take a lot of work to repurpose some existing furniture. Even if you don't consider yourself a DIY'er, there are simple ways to transform something old into a furniture centerpiece. To help you get started, here are my favorite ways to repurpose existing furniture in your home.

Reuse By Changing the Use

The easiest way to repurpose furniture is to use it in a new way. Just because a type of furniture is meant to be used one way, doesn't mean it can't used in a different way.

For example, I think think dressers are one of the most useful pieces of furniture to have. Dressers are intended to be used to hold your clothes, but there are many other ways to use a dresser. In my house we have a dresser in our kitchen for added storage and counter space. I believe you could find a purpose to have a dresser in almost any room. Here are a few ideas of how to repurpose an extra dresser in your home:

- Media center.
- Console table behind a sofa.
- Buffet Cabinet in the dining room.
- To hold office and crafting supplies in a home office.
- Toy storage in a play room.
- Bookcases.

Before you get rid of any furniture, ask yourself if there is any other way you can repurpose this furniture to furnish another room in your home? If you can it think of anyway to use it, search on Pinterest for ideas. If you search, "how to repurpose (fill in the blank)" you will find some amazing ideas. If you really can't reuse something, call me and I will take it off your hands…just don't tell my wife.

Making Over Old Furniture

There are many ways to update a piece of furniture to make it look new again. I would love to refinish furniture everyday. It is so much fun to take furniture from old and ugly to stunning and stylish. All it often takes to make an amazing transformation is a new coat of paint.

It is amazing what a coat of paint can do to an old piece of furniture. I have done this with a few pieces of furniture. Painting a piece of furniture in a bright color can create a beautiful focal point in a room.

You can use a few different types of paint on furniture. By simply using wall paint or spray paint you can create new piece of furniture for just a few dollars. When painting furniture, my preferred method is chalk paint. I will quickly show you how I make, use, and paint furniture with chalk paint to repurpose old discarded pieces of furniture.

Why Chalk Paint?

I would say I was late to the chalk paint craze. The main reason is I did not understand the benefits of chalk paint.

I love refinishing furniture, but like a lot people I hate the prep work that you need to do before you start painting. Who wants or has the time to sand an old stereo cabinet before painting it a beautiful new color to become your new shabby chic tv stand? NOT ME.

I have half a dozen pieces of curbside rescued furniture awaiting me to give them rebirth. However, I never get started because I hate to sand furniture. It is no fun, it's messy, and it's too loud for me to do early in the morning. I usually get up at 4:00 AM to work on decorating projects, while my wife and daughters are still sleeping.

When I finally learned that one of the benefits of chalk paint was that you don't have to sand, I was like sign me up...I can finally work on some furniture projects.

Benefits of Chalk Paint That I Didn't Know

- **Low, Low, VOC'***s* - Chalk Paint has virtually no smell or VOC's which means it is healthier to use in your home.

- **No Need To Sand** - As I said, no need to sand to remove existing finishes, it can even go over a wax finish previously applied.

- **No Priming** - You can skip the priming step, which is time consuming and adds more costs to your DIY project.

- **No Need to Seal with Polyurethane** - After you apply 1 to 2 coats of chalk paint, unlike with latex paint, you don't need to deal with a protective polyurethane coat. It is recommended to apply a coat of finishing wax, which is a lot easier to apply than polyurethane.

- **Dries Fast** - Coats of chalk paint dry fast. You can save time between coats, as it is usually best to do 2 coats.

- **Paint Over Almost Anything** - You can use chalk paint on almost any surface; wood, laminate, metals, plastic, glass, AND even fabric.

I was so excited to test out chalk paint after I found out the amazing benefits. However, there is one disadvantage that I had to overcome, but the good news for you is I discover a solution to this drawback. The main disadvantage I see is the cost.

The most popular brand, Annie Sloan, costs on average $36 for a quart. This is about double the cost of a quart of standard latex paint…ouch!

However, when you factor in the time and money savings by not having to sand, prime or seal; the cost is more reasonable. Also, there are other chalk paint brands that are very good too that cost less.

Two other brands to try are: Americana Decor and Amy Howard at Home.

Another thing that helps with the cost is a quart goes a long way. Depending on the piece of furniture you are painting, it is likely you may have some leftover to use on something else.

So don't let the cost keep you from trying out chalk paint. There are also some DIY recipes for making your own chalk paint from latex paint. This is how I lower the cost of chalk paint. Here is a the recipe I recommend using:

DIY Chalk Paint Recipe

- 1 Cup Plaster of Paris
- 1 Cup Hot Water
- 1-1/2 Cup Latex Paint (using flat paint is best)
- Bowl or Mixing Bucket (I used a mason jar)

1. Mix the hot water and Plaster of Paris first, whisk together until all the Plaster of Paris has dissolved.

2. Then add the paint and mix until all the ingredients are mixed throughly.

Steps to Follow to When Making Over Furniture with Chalk Paint

Step One - Clean Your Furniture Piece

It is important, as with any painting project, that before applying the first coat of paint is to clean the furniture. This helps ensure that the paint adheres to the surface properly and that the surface is smooth.

I simply used soap and water to clean the dirt and dust off furniture.

Step Two - Start Painting

This is my favorite step because you finally get to start seeing the transformation of something ugly into a something beautiful and new.

When painting furniture, make long brush strokes in the same direction to help avoid brush marks.

Hint: Place your furniture legs on blocks or tacks to lift the legs off the ground to make them easier to paint.

This table look much better even after one coat of paint.

Step Three - Add a Second Coat

If you still see brushstrokes after the first coat, don't worry because the second coat will help get rid of those marks.

Chalk paint dries pretty fast. I waited until the next day to do a second coat because of limited time. However, you usually can be safe to paint another coat after an hour.

What I love about chalk paint is the matte and soft finish it has.

Step Four - Wax On

This might be the most intimidating step for first time chalk painters. However, let me ease your worries about this step.

Waxing…is FUN and EASY!

Waxing is a lot easier than sealing furniture with polyurethane. With polyurethane there is so much more room for mistakes. With wax, if you put too much wax on, you simply buff it off.

So here is how you apply the wax.

Using a bristle brush or lint free rag, apply a thin layer of wax over all the surfaces. Since I was using clear wax, I found it to be hard to see where I had already applied wax. So I recommend starting on the top and working your way down.

Once you have applied wax to your piece of furniture, let it dry for an hour.

Step Five - Time To Buff

Buffing is the final step to this furniture makeover. Using a lint free rag, begin wiping the surfaces gently.

As you do this you will notice a nice satin finish and shine appear. Continue to buff until all the excess wax has been removed and the finish looks even.

Do you see the shine?

At this point you are done, unless you want to apply another wax coat for more protection. Two to three coats of wax are recommend for high use furniture. If you add another coat repeat steps 4 & 5.

That is all it takes to repurpose existing furniture with chalk paint. Less expensive than buying new furniture and so much better for many reasons. I challenge you to test your hands at repainting a piece of furniture next time you are decorating your home.

Here are two of my furniture makeovers:

Pedestal Table Makeover

Stereo Cabinet Makeover

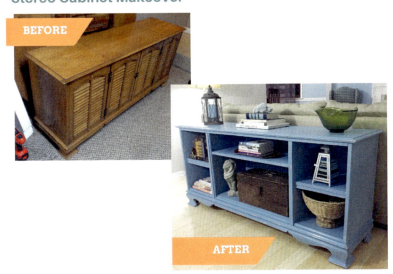

Repurposing Common Items

Repurposing is not just for furniture. You can repurpose many common items to furnish your home for less. Simple, everyday items that you may discard, often make beautiful decorative objects to personalize your shelves, walls, tables and counters. Plus, one of the added benefits to using everyday items is they are inexpensive or you may already have them. Which, if you are decorating on a limited budget, is really important.

Anytime you do not need to buy something new to furnish your home saves you money.

Some everyday items can easily be repurposed or upcycled into new decor. To help you start looking at everything as a possible decorative item, here is a list of common items that can transform your home's decor.

Wooden Ladders - wooden ladders are very versatile common items. You can do a number of things with a ladder...hang it from the ceiling to hang pots and pans, as a magazine holder, and my personal favorite, as a towel holder in your bathroom.

Dishes & Glassware - if you have open shelves in your kitchen, displaying your dishes, bowls, mugs and other glassware becomes the decor in your kitchen. If this is the situation in your kitchen, get dishware with color for an instant accent.

Plates or Platters - antique or China plates or platters hung on the wall adds a focal point in a dining room.

Trays - food trays are fantastic multi-use items for your home. Place a tray with a few books and accessories to dress up a coffee table or bathroom counter.

This is tray in my bathroom that organizes some items.

Books - books you already have can be used to decorate shelves and counters. Create small stacks of interesting books to place on shelves or console tables.

This is just one place in my home I used books to decorate a table.

Vintage Anything - vintage items are wonderful to keep and have on hand when decorating. Vintage cameras, typewriters, or other small objects are interesting to mix in with new items. If you do not have any vintage items see if your parents or grandparents have anything you can have.

This vintage lantern and hand wood planers are some of my favorite decorative items because they belonged to my wife's papa.

Purses - for the guys that read my blog this is not for you...ladies if you have a collection of purses and handbags, display them altogether on floating shelves or on wall hooks. Not only will this give your purses a dual purpose...you will also be able to find your favorite handbag a lot faster.

Jewelry - sorry guys one more for the ladies...display your jewelry altogether in your bathroom, bedroom or walk-in closet.

Cake Stands - cake stands are great for elevating other decor to create different layers...which is a key to styling any space.

Mason Jars - Mason jars are very popular these days because they are so versatile and add a rustic and somewhat industrial feel to a room. You can use Mason jars as vases, candles holders, and even as a pendant light.

Hand Mirrors, Perfume Bottles, & Brushes - in your bathroom display a nice tray of perfumes bottles, a nice hand mirror and hair brush can give the room a simple sense of elegance.

Luggage - if you have old luggage that you are no longer using repurpose it as inexpensive decor. You can also store items in the luggage to hide clutter. There are also many ideas out there on ways to recreate old luggage into end tables, liquor storage, bookshelves, etc.

Wood Utensils - wood kitchen utensils, if you don't have any you can pick up some cheaply at a thrift store. Wood utensils are great for dressing up your kitchen counter. Place them in a utensils jar to create quick and functional decor in your kitchen.

Maps - frame old maps from your glove compartment or cut maps out of a world atlas. A large map creates an interesting focal point in a room.

Rope - natural rope can be used in many ways to decorate. You can wrap jute rope around a mason jar or vase. Here is a example of a quick and simple why I used some jute rope to accent my fireplace mantle:

Sports Equipment - if you are stumped on how to decorate your kids room…display their sports equipment. Skateboards, baseball bats and gloves, hockey sticks, skis, etc. make great decor in a teens room. Same thing can be done with musical instruments.

Doors or Shutters - old doors or shutters painted in an accent color and hung on the wall is a cheap way to add artwork to a room.

Architectural or Industrial Items - fancy moldings, old pulleys, gears, or tools are the perfect items to style a shelf or mantle. Clean these items a little bit, but not too much because you want their age to show.

Scrap Wood - I keep and collect a lot of scrap wood. Scrap wood can be used in many ways to decorate your home. You can stencil or transfer words onto the wood to create a personalize wall sign, put several pieces together to make a decorative tray, or if you have enough scrap wood, create a whole wood plank wall.

I made is wood tray completely out of scrap wood, then stained and painted it to give the tray a weathered look.

Stones or Rocks - stones or rocks are great little decorative items you can pick up for free out in your yard. A small stone can top a stack of books on a coffee table. A heavy rock can make a bookend. Stones and rocks are more than just paper weights when it comes to decorating. They bring a connection to nature into your home.

You can save a lot of money repurposing common items. Think of something you can repurpose next time you are decorating.

Repurposing is a Key to Successful Decorating

I can't imagine decorating without repurposing something old. It is almost like that saying for a wedding. "Something old, something blue, something borrowed, and a penny in your shoe." Repurposing makes your decorating successful, interesting, and personal to you. When you repurpose old furniture, especially when it has a story behind it, it gives your home meaning and life. Repurposing items and furniture saves you money, but also helps make a house a home.

> "Always remember that one person's junk is your home furnishing treasure."

Simple decor in a bathroom is ideal for a clean and elegant look.

CHAPTER NINETEEN

Thrifty Ways to Save Money When Decorating

"I'm not cheap, I'm thrifty."
- Kym Whitley

Being thrifty is WAY in. Smart home decorators are hunting for thrifty finds to furnish their homes, to be stylish, and budget-friendly. I have already told you that decorating a home doesn't have to cost as much as your children's college funds. If you are willing to shop smart for deals and do a DIY project you can design a home on a shoestring budget.

To help become a Savvy Thrifty Decorator, here are quick ideas and tricks I have used to decorate my home on less than $15 a month. Regardless of the size of your budget these tips will benefit you.

Stop Buying These Items New

One way to be thrifty is to not buy new. You can save a lot of money buying some of your home furnishing used. I will say, sometimes it is better to buy new…like tires for your car.

However, these home furnishings I recommend buying used. Most of them you should have no problem finding at your nearest thrift store.

Vases

You can find vases at nearly every consignment shop or thrift store. When decorating with vases, my tip is to purchase vases that are at least melon size to make the biggest impact. Also, any clear glass vase can be painted any color to suit the color scheme of your home.

This a $0.99 vase that I chalk painted to work with my color scheme.

Decorative Books

All interior designers use books when decorating a room. They are extremely versatile and you can find used book at many garage sales and Goodwills. I recently pick up some old Reader's Digest Story books for $0.50 each. These look great stacked with a decorative item on top. What you want to look for are books of varying sizes, colorful covers and bindings.

Frames

Never buy frames new, unless you are looking for all the same frame. However, mixing different styles and sizes of frames on a wall creates a great gallery in any room. Remember when looking for frames not to be very concerned with the color of the frames. You can always spray paint the frame to match all the others. Mixing colors on the wall can look stylish, too.

Baskets

Baskets are very useful in your home. You can use them for decorating and to hide items you don't need all the time. You can save money on baskets by not buying baskets new. Save some money from leaving your purse by purchasing baskets at your local thrift store or at garage sales in your neighborhood.

Figurines

A design trend you see for interior decorating is ceramic figurines. Often these items are painted in white or an accent color. If you buy these ceramic figurines new you will pay a premium. You can find old ugly ceramic figurines at nearly all thrift stores. I recently bought a ceramic owl for a $1 that I painted white. I have seen similar white owls for $15 - $25 depending on what home decor store you go to. Save some money by buying ugly and turning into extraordinary.

I thought this owl was scary looking, but after spray painting, it's now a stylish & not tacky.

Lamps

Lighting is extremely important for all rooms of your home. However, lighting fixtures are an expensive item when furnishing a space. Table lamps sometimes are a little hard to find at thrift stores, but if you are a frequent shopper like I am you will see old lamps that can look amazing in your home after a little TLC. You can usually pick up a good lamp for between $3 - $10 at Goodwill. Spray paint an outdated table lamp a fun color and add a new lamp shade to create a modern redo of something old. Here is an example of brass lamps I made over.

I have these two brass table lamps, as you can see one of them I have chalk painted white and got a $0.50 burlap shade that I added a teal burlap to, which fits into my living room color scheme.

Side Tables

Side tables are excellent items to buy used because you can readily find them at used furniture stores. Plus, like many used and old home furnishings, they can be easily updated with a fresh coat of paint. If you are trying to track down a pair of side tables but can't find matching ones, don't be afraid to mix and match. Diversity in a room creates interest and a unique style.

Buying used is just one way to be thrifty decorating. Here are some other simple ways to be frugal when furnishing your home.

Thrifty Money Saving Tips

- **Garage Sale Hunting** - my wife and I really like to go out on Saturday mornings looking for great deals at garage sales. I am always on the hunt for quality furniture, home accessories, and artwork. *Tip*: if you have several items you want, group them together and offer a lump sum price. Also, go to garage sales towards the end of day for better deals.

- **The Dollar Store is Your Friend** - believe it or not but there are a number of excellent home decorating accessories at the Dollar Store, such as; frames, candles, vases, baskets, and more.

- **Empty Frames for Instant Artwork** - No money for artwork? Group empty frames on one wall to create a cheap and easy focal point in any room. Use different styles, sizes, shapes and either paint them all one color or leave them as is.

- **Rearrange Before Buying New** - sometimes simply rearranging the furniture can restyle a room to make a new statement. Moving furniture can create a new focal point in the room, such as around a fireplace, television or exterior view. You can also take furniture from one room to bring into another room to create a different look. Just by moving or rearranging the furniture pieces in a room can help save money.

- **Paint a Bold Color** - color can dramatically change a room. Color creates a new mood for a space. Instead of repainting a whole room, try painting one focal wall a bold accent color. Paint is an inexpensive way to reinvent your home's decor.

- **Use Nature to Accessorize your Home** - go to your backyard and bring things from nature into your home. Leafless twigs in a vase, fresh cut flowers, or fall leaves are free accessories that can bring a sense of nature's beauty into your home. You can also take pictures of flowers to frame in a grouping to bring the outdoors inside.

- **Ask Friends and Family for their Unused Furniture** - many people have unused furniture in basements or storage garages. Post on Facebook what you are looking and maybe one of your friends will have a hand-me-down piece of furniture for free or cheap. I have several pieces of furniture that have found a new home in my house from family and friends. It can't hurt to ask and you will be surprised what you find.

This beautiful armoire I got for free from a friend and neighbor. It needs a makeover but right now it works perfect to organize my wife's home school materials.

- **Variety is the Spice of Life & Decor** - in nature, there is no two trees that are exactly alike. You can apply nature's example of diversity into your home to save money. If you need a pair of chairs or lamps you can find two items that don't match. Mixing pairs of furniture will give your home an interesting, one-of-a-kind, eclectic style. It is often easier and less expensive to find two different lamps at a garage sale or thrift store.

- **Shop for Scratch & Dent Specials** - if you are looking for new cabinets or appliances for your kitchen, you can save money by accepting some minor scratches or dents. Often times the scratch or dent is on the back or sides where no one will notice it.

- **Shop at Liquidation Stores for Flooring** - shopping at liquidation stores helps make flooring more affordable. I personally bought bamboo flooring for my home at over half off by shopping at a liquidation flooring store. Often you can get a much higher quality wood flooring for less than the lesser quality flooring you were considering.

- **Reupholstering an Accent Chair** - it you have a sofa or chair you love, but the upholstery is either worn out or out of date, reupholstering that piece can be less expensive than buying something new. Depending on the fabric you choose, a 6-7 foot sofa can cost $500-$800 to reupholster. This is a good savings when an average new sofa can cost you $1200 or more.

This was a very inexpensive chair to reupholstered. I use less than a yard of strap fabric I had and new foam cushion I got at a garage sale to transform this curbside find into a beautiful chair again.

- **Find Your Inner Photographer** - one way to inexpensively add art to your home to is display your own photography. For instance, I recently took photos of flowers in my backyard. A grouping a three or more similar themed photos are a perfect dressing for a wall.

- **Make Your Own Custom Frames** - no money for custom frames? Make your own custom frames for artwork in the home without any power tools. Head on over *A Beautiful Mess* to read Mandi's post Build a Custom Frame No Power Tools Required, check is post out by going to www.decoratingwithless.com/

mandi. She has a wonderful method of creating custom inexpensive frames. Her methods are much more cost saving when framing odd sized artwork.

- **Add Color with a Bowl of Fruit** - a clear glass bowl of fruit is a simple and quick way to add a splash of color in a room. Before you eat your oranges, lemons, limes, or apples, display them on a shelf.

- **Art Swap with Your Friends** - you may have artwork in your home that you have had forever and have grown tired of. Before you go out and buy new art, ask your family and friends if they would want to swap wall art with you. Most likely they have art on their walls they are just as sick of, which would look perfect in your home.

- **Shop at the Right Stores** - instead of shopping at the designer stores, buy home accessories at discount stores. My favorite stores to shop at are Homegoods, Marshalls, and Tuesday Morning. You can often find good deals on art, vases, baskets, throw blankets, pillows, small furniture and decor.

- **Think Neutral When Shopping for a Sofa** - If you are buying a new sofa or other upholstered furniture consider going with a neutral fabric. A neutral upholstered sofa can be accessorized with any color or style. If you are going to spend money on new furniture, neutral fabric will stand the test of trends and time.

- **Shop at the End of a Season or Holiday** - you can save money on home accessories and decor if you wait until the end of a season or holiday. Most retailers will markdown their out of season decor as much as 50% off which is good for the frugal decorator.

- **Inexpensive Knock-Offs** - have you ever fallen in love with that perfect accessory and looked at the price tag and cried. I've been there. If you are willing to get a little creative and use your hands you can often times make your own home decor knock-offs. One of my favorite blogs to follow is Beckie Farrant's KnockOffDecor.com. She features tutorials of the best knock-offs for your home. No one will know the difference and you will have more money in your purse for other home accessories.

- **Think Simple** - in my opinion decorating with less or more simplicity is the best way to save money on home decor. To save money, take a less is more approach when decorating your home. Look at each room in your house and see what is the minimal furniture and decor you need to decorate the space. Just because you have 4 walls doesn't mean that all 4 walls need something. Choose 1 or 2 walls you want to be your focal walls. If your room is already decorated try removing items until you have the amount of decor that feels comfortable without feeling empty.

- **Orange Clearance Tags** - They may be a different color at the store you shop at, but keep your eye out for clearance tags and stickers. You can save big on mark downed home accessories at big groceries stores. For instance, I once saved over $18 on a new shower curtain. That was AWESOME!

Being Thrifty = Money in Your Pocket

For me, being thrifty is second nature. I use these tips all of the time because I need to stretch my decorating budget as far as possible. I hope you have found a few of these thrifty ideas helpful. The biggest thing is home decorating should be fun and not cost you a fortune. Your interior design dreams can come true for any budget if you get a little creative and think outside the box. Try some of these thrifty money saving tips to keep more money in your pocket, while still furnishing your home in style.

Now it is time to start the final step…Style.

Flowers are an easy way to add a pop of color in any room.

CHAPTER TWENTY

Step #4 Style: Finishing Touches & a Few Tweaks

"If shoes are the finishing touches to any outfit, then well styled home accessories are the finishing touches that make a good room into a great one"
- Matthew Iacopelli

You made it! We are in the home stretch of decorating your home to be great. There are just a few finishing touches and final tweaks to make. I know your home is probably looking better than it has ever looked. It would be easy to be finished now, but these final actions do make a difference.

What is left in this book is like the icing on a cake. It is needed to give a room a designer look. You have come so far, I don't want you to settle for good, when great is just a few steps away. Are you to ready to finally have a room fully design and ready for the before and after comparison? Here is what's next.

Lighting Your Space

Beyond the need to be able to see your way through a room at night, lighting is an important and sometimes overlooked step to decorating your home. Much like colors, lighting can have a positive or negative affect on how we feel. So having the right lighting is vital in designing a stunning room.

In the chapter 21, *Highlighting & Accenting a Space with Lighting*, I will show you how to add three types of lighting to any room. When done right, your home will look amazing regardless of what time of day it is.

Styling With Home Accessories

Have you ever fallen in love with how perfectly accessorized rooms look in home decor magazines? I know I have. Do you have trouble with recreating the same look in your home? Styling your home with accessories may seem like an impossible dream.

However, it is possible for you to get that designer look without a designer. Don't believe me?

In chapter 22, *Styling Your Home with Meaningful Finishing Touches*, I will share with you 7 tips to help you style your home like a pro. It is easier than you may think to add stylish home accessories and make a meaningful to home. With these tips, you will now know how to style fireplace mantles, console and coffee tables, and any other place you want to add a little finishing touch and style.

Some Final Tweaks

Have you ever finished a project and something just seems off? Sometimes this happens when you are finished decorating a room. You step back, it looks great, but something seems amiss. Don't be worried if this happens. You didn't do anything wrong. There maybe just a few final tweaks to make everything feel just right.

In chapter 23, *Small Tweaks that Make a Big Difference*, I will show you some last minutes tweaks to make to your design that will help it shine. These tweaks are quick and easy ways to take your home up a notch so everything you have worked so hard to do will pay off.

Let's keep on going together and finish this amazing journey of transformation in style.

CHAPTER TWENTY-ONE

Highlighting & Accenting a Space with Lighting

"A room is never complete without layers of good lighting – of course it must be functional, but be sure to also include decorative choices for ambiance. Make a statement in a space with unique chandeliers, sconces, or lamps – great lighting is the always frosting on the cake."
– Kate Riley, Centsational Girl

Lighting is an important element in decorating a room. Not only does lighting add illumination to a room, but it can also add style and interest. Often people make the mistake of not thinking about the way they place lighting in a room. Lighting adds drama to a room. Lighting can change the look and feel of a space. Dark rooms feel unwelcoming. My daughter Hannah won't go into a room that isn't lit. Rooms with balanced lighting are inviting and warm to be in.

Creating the balance and layering lighting can be tricky. However, I have a few tips to help make styling your home with light much easier.

What's Going On

If you want to light a room properly, the first thing you have to think about is what activities happen in the space. Lighting is needed for activities to happen. If the lighting is wrong it can be difficult to do certain activities. Just think of how hard it is to get around when the power goes out or to dress in the dark, which I often have to do to not wake Lynn up in the morning.

Different activities require different types and levels of lighting. Most rooms will have three types of lighting: *general*, *task*, and *accent*. These three types, layered together, create a well lit room that can be lit differently through the day. Having all three types also makes a room more versatile and able to function for multiple activities.

How to Use Each Type of Lighting

To make lighting easy for you, here is how to use each lighting type in a space.

General

General lighting refers to light that evenly lights a room. Some rooms with ample natural light will often not need general lighting; natural daylight lighting is my favorite type of light. However, not all rooms get enough natural light. Often overhead ceiling fixtures provide general light for a room.

Many newer or renovated homes use recessed can lights to create even overhead light. Other options for general lighting are flush mount and semi-flush fixtures, ceiling fans, and chandeliers. Chandeliers also can help create zones in a room by defining an area.

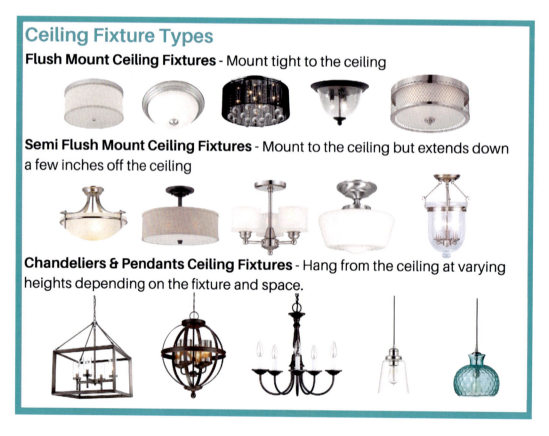

If you have a room like my living room with no overhead lighting, large floor lamps can be placed in the space. If you are looking for a floor lamp a great option is an arched floor lamps because it creates a zone and acts similar to a ceiling fixture.

One more thing about general lighting is it is the least intense lighting in a room when you are layering in all three types.

Task

Task lighting is the light need to illuminate any area where a specific task is performed. A frequent activity that requires task lighting is reading a good book. A table or floor lamp next to your favorite cozy reading chair will work great for task lighting. Other areas in your home where you may need task lighting are a desk, crafting table, and kitchen counter. Task lighting is more directed and intense lighting.

Accent

To put the finishing touches on a successful lighting design is accent lighting. You will always want to choose an area to accent with lighting. One item you may choose to accent is artwork on the wall. This can be done by using a special artwork light fixture or track lighting. You can use accent lighting to enhance your focal point in the room.

Tips to Brighten a Dark Room

We all have rooms in our homes that are dark. My living room in the front of the house is a dark room. No one wants to hang out in a room that feels like a cave. To avoid having a cave like room, here are tips to help make a dark room brighter.

Add a Pale Color Area Rug

A large pale colored rug will draw guests' eyes from the dark walls and into the overall space. In addition, materials with lighter hues will reflect more light around the room.

Mirrors are a Dark Room's Best Friend

I love adding mirrors to a room for many reasons. One reason is mirrors will reflect natural and artificial light throughout a room. The ideal placement of a mirror in a dark room is opposite or perpendicular to a window. Placing a large mirror in one of these locations will maximize the amount of light projected into the room.

Add Lighting

A simple way you can make a dark room brighter is by adding lighting fixtures to the room. Ideally you will want to add lighting that casts light up and down. Wall sconces, floor and table lamps with shades that are open at the top and bottom are perfect to lighten a room. For renters, you can purchase wall sconces you can install without running cables behind the wall.

Add Some Bling

Adding reflective accessories is a great way to brighten up a room without paint. Metallic furnishings or items with a glossy finish reflect more light than accessories with matte or flat finishes. Plus, metallics are a big interior design trend. Add some gold or silver into your decor to brighten your room and add style.

Metallic candlesticks are one easy way to add accessories to brighten a room.

White, White, White

Avoid dark finishes, pale grays and warms colors. White accents, such as white curtains, vases and furniture, contrast against dark paint colors which will help brighten your room. Dark furnishings absorb more light than white accessories, so reducing dark finishes is a key to brightening a dark room.

Pops of Bright Colors

To avoid going too sterile with all white furnishings, add some pops of bright colors to break up the neutral background. Don't be afraid of adding color, use primary or jewel tone colors.

Light Woods

Light wood tones will also help you lighten a dark room. Natural maple or cherry are a great choice.

Large Art Wall

Large artwork can be an expensive but effective way of lighten a room without changing paint color. If you don't have the budget for large artwork, consider adding a wide white matting around smaller art to give it a brighter impact on the space.

Plants

Plants add life and color to a dark room. Plants are important in home decor for so many reasons, including bringing nature indoors and improving indoor air quality.

Paint Your Walls A Lighter Color

Painting a dark room a lighter color will transform the room. I did this in my dark living room and it has lightened up the space dramatically. Even simply painting one wall a lighter color can help.

Lighting your home shouldn't be difficult. The biggest thing to remember is to consider what happens in the room and light the space to make that activity easy to do. Simply remember G.T.A. when adding lighting: *General, Task, Accent.* Layer in these three types of lighting to create a dramatically lit space that is interesting and inviting.

CHAPTER TWENTY-TWO

Styling Your Home with Meaningful Finishing Touches

"Style is a way to say who you are without having to speak."
- Rachel Zoe

Have you ever looked longingly at a home decor magazine and wished you could style your home like a professional interior designer?

Let me tell you that as an interior designer, I look at these photos and wish the same thing at times. My home is more of the real-life variety than magazine home on most days, which is perfect for me.

What if I told you that with a few easy steps you could style your home like a designer. It is possible and you can make your home look more photo ready by following a simple decorating formula.

These 7 steps apply to any place in your home; bookshelves, console tables, dressers, counters, etc. that you want to accessorize.

Styling to Create a Meaningful Home

As the quote at the beginning of this chapter says, style is what tells others who you are without saying a word. Your home decor should express you. How do you express yourself in home decor? Simple, add accessories that have special meaning to you. Now sure you can buy new decor to style your home with, but don't be afraid to decorate with meaningful personal items and treasures.

For instance, in our master bedroom I have on my dresser the wedding cake topper from our wedding. This item has great meaning for Lynn and I. It reminds us of the day we became husband and wife. We can share the story of our wedding with our family and friends by displaying this personal item.

We have a purple shot glass candle holder from the college dance that Lynn and I meet for the first time.

You can also style with meaning by making your own home decor. Not only can you tell people how you made it, but you will have pride in what you created. Lastly, when you buy new decor, buy accessories that speak to your likes. We love the beach so many items in our home are beach inspired. When someone comes into our home we want them to feel relaxed like we do when we go to the beach.

What is Styling Your Home?

Styling your home is what I call the icing on the cake. It is the finishing touches that complete the design to make it unique, add character, color, texture, and define a style or theme.

Designers use accessories to style homes. These accessories often consist of accent pillows, decorative objects, wall art, plants, flowers, and baskets or storage boxes.

The art of combining these items in a room is what styling your home is all about. And doing this may seems like rocket science but it is not. Follow the guide I use when styling my home to create a designer look to your home.

1. Choose a Focal Piece

The first step to styling an area in your home is selecting a focal piece. This centerpiece will anchor the overall arrangement of home accessories.

What makes a good focal piece? Generally your focal piece is something larger in scale.

The mirror over this dining room buffet is the focal point in this vignette.

Collection can also make a beautiful focal piece, instead of having a single item.

Most often the focal piece is placed in the center of the arrangement.

2. Pay Attention to Crowd Control

Step two is crowd control. I have seen rooms that are packed with so many knick knacks and mementos that you cannot even see the counter. When you begin accessorizing a room, pare down your furnishing to your favorite items. The number of home accessories will vary depending on what you are styling.

For instance, you will need less decorative items to style a console table than a whole built-in bookshelf. However, in general, my suggestion is to leave 25% to 50% of negative space. Negative space is key to create spaces that looks professionally designed. So don't be afraid to leave space between items or shelves half empty.

Also, remember that too much of a good thing, like too many accessories, is a bad thing. Paring down your home accessories will make your home styling look less cluttered and haphazard.

3. Create Groupings of Accessories

Step three in styling your home like a pro is creating groupings of accessories. Whether you are decorating a console table, bookshelf, or wall, creating small groupings of home accessories is key.

What do you use in your groupings? Well you may not like my answer...**anything**. I know that doesn't seem like much help does it. Let me explain this further to make grouping easy.

When you look at professionally designed rooms, the accessories used to create groupings varies completely from one group to the next.

However, items that work well to create interesting groupings are books, vases, figurines, candle sticks, trays, fruit, small framed art or photos. Mixing accessories creates interesting vignettes that will give your home a designer look.

A key point to remember when styling is there should be an overall connecting theme between your home furnishings.

4. Add Accessories Varying in Height

When styling your home, another designer tip is adding accessories with varying heights. Blend in objects that are tall and short to add interest and character.

Adding items that are taller will draw your eyes, and shorter accessories will keep your eyes at one level. Mixing tall and short objects draw your eye around the whole area, making your styling a focal point in the room.

Candlesticks in three heights make adding varying levels easy as pie.

5. Layering

The fifth step to styling like a pro is to layer your home decor. Similar to varying the height, overlapping and layering accessories creates a dramatic arrangement.

Don't worry if some items are partially covered by another item, this is the idea. By layering your decor you create interest, depth and an overall vignette that looks pleasing to the eye.

6. Add Some Color

Home accessories are an ideal way to infuse some color into a room. So when styling your home, add accessories in a color or colors that coordinate with your overall color scheme.

The blue candle on the coffee table tray add a pop of color to this vignette.

Now every decorative item doesn't have to be a color, in fact it is better if not everything is a color. This goes back to the key of adding variety…variety is the spice of life.

As you style, blend together accessories with accents colors and others that are neutral with no color. Remember I covered how only 10% of a room's color should come from the accent color and 90% comes from the main and secondary colors.

When accessorizing, remember 10% accent color to help you avoid adding too much of a good thing.

7. Add Lighting

Adding lighting when styling a room is sometimes an optional step. Depending on what and where you are decorating you may not need lighting or have room for a lamp.

For instance, adding a lamp in a bookcase may be difficult because of size. However, if you are styling a console table you could consider placing a lamp on one or both ends of table. Lamps will add height and if you use two lamps on either end it will create symmetry and balance.

BONUS TIP

A good way to not get bored with your home accessories is to change or swap around the accessories throughout the year, perhaps quarterly, to give your home a fresh new look.

I know I get tired of my home accessories throughout the year, and have a desire for change. Buying new decor every time I get bored with how things look would get expensive.

By swapping around home decor instead of buying new accessories I save money and you can do the same.

Time to Get Styling Your Home!

Styling your home like the a pro is not impossible. It is just a matter of knowing the right steps and how to arrange home accessories in an interesting way. In the end when you follow these easy steps the results will be an exquisite focal point in your home.

I hope these tips help you when you are decorating your home or apartment. With this guide you can now style anything in your home and everyone will think you had professional help. Now you are ready to make a few final tweaks to take your home decorating from good to great!

CHAPTER TWENTY-THREE

Small Tweaks that Make a Big Difference

"Have no fear of perfection - you'll never reach it."
- Salvador Dali

For me, home decorating is an ongoing process; it is never perfect. But perfection is not what I am striving for. It is important to find beauty in imperfection. However, when you are just about done with decorating a room, you may feel that something is not quite right. This is a common feeling, so don't worry if you feel this way. You haven't done anything wrong. To make the room feeling right, you may want to make a few small tweaks. Small changes can make a big difference.

10 Final Decorating Tweaks

These quick and easy tweaks can help your decorating shine.

Rearrange Home Accessories

I rearrange home accessories all the time until I feel the styling is just right. Don't be afraid to try tweaking your accessories if something seems incomplete. Like to trade items in and out throughout the year to keep the look fresh and interesting. I have a cabinet in my basement where I "shop" from when I ready to tweak something. Shopping from my own decor also helps me save money.

Switch Around Furniture

Sometimes switching around the furniture layout can help change the look and make it complete. You can test out flip-flopping accent chairs to create a new look. Or steal a chair from another room to finish the space. Also, if those tweaks don't work, remove a chair to see if that makes things better.

Soften Things Up

If a room has too many hard lines, such as modern style furniture, add throw blankets to soften the room. Simple ways to add blankets to a room are hung over an arm of a sofa or in a nice basket. Blankets add a welcoming cozy feel to a room.

Fresh Flowers

A simple tweak that adds a lot to a space is fresh cut flowers. Flowers add color, life, and beauty to your home. It would be expensive to but flowers every week though. To make it easy and less expensive, plant wildflowers, perennials, or your favorite type of flower in your yard. This way throughout the summer you can always have quick access to fresh flowers.

Edit, Edit, Edit

If something seems off when you finish decorating, maybe it's time to edit. Less is more. Simplifying whats in a room can make the important elements of the design stand out. You can test this out by removing items that seems to be distracting. Another way to determine what to edit is to remove all the accessories from the room. Then slowly add accessories back in, stopping when the room looks right.

Set the Table

A bare dining table looks odd and boring. To complete a dining room makeover, set and style the table. I love table runners, so add a table runner with a centerpiece to start. Next, set the table with placemats and plates to add a welcoming finishing touch. Not only will it look amazing, but it will also help keep your dining table from becoming a catch all, which happens in my home.

Light Some Candles

Candles add a sense of warmth, romance, and aroma to a room. If your bedroom or living room feels incomplete, place some candles somewhere in the room. I like grouping three candles together to maximize their affect on the room.

House Plants

Adding house plants is a final tweak that has benefits beyond adding color. Indoor plants help indoor air quality, keep you healthy, and have been known to make people feel more happy. If you are like me and have problems keeping house plants alive, here are 5 low maintenance plants for us brown thumb people.

- Jade
- Aloe
- Snake Plant
- Heart Leaf Philodendron
- ZZ Plant

All these plants are hardy, but if you still are scare to put live plants in your home there is still an option. Artificial plant have come a long way and look almost ideal to their live counterparts.

Not sure where to put plants in your home? Here are some good places for plants:

- On shelves.
- Hanging from a ceiling.
- On a side or console table.

- On the kitchen counter.
- In a corner of the room.

You can also add style with the type of pots you use. Just be sure you read up on the type of plant you add so you understand how much water and sunlight it needs to thrive.

If you have pets, be sure you make sure your house plants are not toxic to your four-legged friends.

I got this spider plant from a good friend. Now it is on a shelf in my dining room.

Linens and Things

A tweak that can be used in a bathroom or kitchen is changing out or adding new towels and linens. I am not a big fan of theming my decor for each holiday. It is a lot of work and money. I think when a it comes to holiday decorations, a little can go long way. However, adding patterned hand towels and linens is a quick way to add a finishing touch to complete a room. Test it out, buy some new hand towels for a bathroom. Before removing the sale tags, place them in the your bathroom and see if they help finish the look.

Pick two colors that work with your color scheme and get a hand and bath towels in those colors. Then layer a hand and bath towel together.

Change Nothing & Enjoy

If something seems off or incomplete, do nothing. I know it sounds weird to say that. I know when I see something that is bothering me my immediate reaction is to fix it. However, sometimes it is better to wait a few days or a week before making any changes. When you finish a room you can be overly critical. If you are the decorator in your house, you see things differently than others in your home. Things you see as wrong or a mistake, others won't notice. Like wine, sometimes letting the design breathe and get lived in makes the room feel complete.

Remember, home decorating is a fluid process. Adding and tweaking a room is common when a room is "done." Also, I find tweaking a room throughout the year helps me not get bored with the space. When you find yourself at the end of decorating a room, don't be afraid to tweak things a little. I don't recommend doing all ten of these tweaks. However, trying out one or two of these that work for your home can help make a big difference.

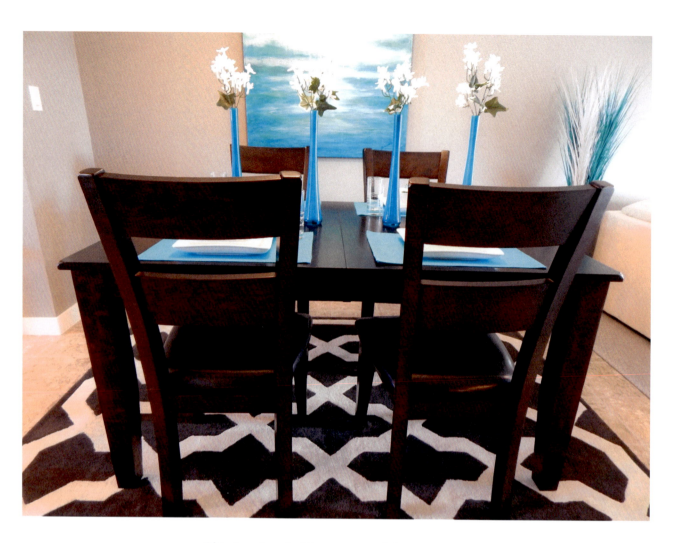

This is a lovely blue accented dining room.

CHAPTER TWENTY-FOUR

Putting in All Together

"Step by step and the thing is done."
- Charles Atlas

Congratulations! You're are ready to make a big transformation in your home. The fact that you have made it this far shows that you do have what it takes to decorate your home the way you have always hope for. You are not interested in letting another year, month or week go by without making tangible steps toward achieving your goals. You've got this! And I believe in you. Sometimes all it takes is a little encouragement and guidance to make a big difference.

We've covered a ton of material about home decorating, but I don't want to leave to you without an action plan.

1. Print off the Home Decorating Success Roadmap. If you have not already done so, I strongly encourage you to print off the *Home Decorating Success Roadmap*. It is a great reminder of the 4 decorating steps you learned about in this book. I even printed off the PDF and hung it next to my desk. I see it everyday and it helps me remember what steps to take each day. You can get your own copy by going to: DecoratingWithLess.com/bonus.

2. Take small steps everyday. Remember that home decorating is a journey, not something that happens overnight. That being said, you now know the path. For now decide what step you are on in the roadmap. Remember, it is not a race. I am still on this journey with you. I encourage to take your time. Decorating your home is about taking small steps everyday. Even 15 minutes a day overtime will have big results. Each day try to work on some aspect of the journey. Sometimes there are bumps a long the way and mistakes made, but don't get discouraged. Everything is solvable and fixable. Take a small step back to regroup and start again. You can do this!

3. Remember to have fun. Home decorating is about having fun. Sure there are some struggles. But you now have the right mindset about decorating. You have what is takes, you know that it doesn't have to be perfect, and that you can decorate your home on any budget. So have fun! There is so much enjoyment in creating a beautiful home for your family. Have fun with the process.

4. Join The Design Studio. Have you ever wished to you had access to an interior designer throughout the year to help you decorate your home, ask questions, get advice, and be encouraged by other people that are passionate about home decorating? I bet the answer is YES! That is why I started the Design Studio (DS). DS is a community of people like yourself that are passionate about home decorating. Now that you have read the book, you can experience a deeper dive inside of DS. Home decorating concepts that are difficult to explain in a book.

Inside the Design Studio, I walk you through the decorating concepts and advice in a visual format so you can have a better understanding of how to transform you space. DS members also will have access to me to get advice, exclusive live regularly schedule classes along with open design consultation calls. Now, I only open the doors to Home Decorating Design Studio a few times a year. To find out more go to DecoratingWithLess.com/DesignStudio.

Closing Thoughts

A lot can change as you decorate your home. Home decorating has a strong affect not only on your physical environment, but also on a psychological level, too. In my personal experience, decorating has made me a happier person. I feel excited when I come home because I have pride in the home that I have created for my family. I hope you will experience unexpected positive results from decorating your home.

One surprise for my wife and I is we are more content with our home. We were planning on moving in a year, but now after seeing the results we are considering staying in our current home longer. The joy of designing a home to fit your needs and style will add so much to your life. HGTV's show, *Love It or List It*, is a perfect example of the contentment people can have after their home is made over. A house they once hated, they now love again. Home decorating can help you fall in love with your home again, too.

Here are few other thoughts I want to leave you with.

Believe in yourself, goals, and dreams for your home even when other don't. A beautiful home is worth the hard work, blood, sweat, and tears. I know it is easy to second guess or get down on your ideas and dreams. However, don't let negative self-talk stop you from decorating. Kick the resistance to the curb, and if you need to, decorate afraid, but get started. Your dreams are within your grasp and you can achieve your goals.

Find a community to support you. One thing I know for sure is that nothing helps you get through struggles or celebrate a win like finding a community that believes in you and shares your passion for home decorating. Thanks to Facebook, it is easier than ever to find a community to cheer you on and help you keep going. If you can't find a community come join our closed DWL Community Group where we have a growing group of passionate home decorators that will cheer you on your journey. To join head over to DecoratingWithLess.com/DWLgroup.

I am so excited to watch you transform your home. I will continue to share my home's transformation as I am on this journey with you. Together we can help each chase our dreams. *It starts today!*

About The Author

Matthew Iacopelli is a busy Interior Designer, Décor Blogger, husband, and father of two beautiful girls. Since 2008, he has practiced interior design professionally designing both commercial and residential projects across the country and the world.

After 5 years as an interior designer, Matthew decided to started blogging about home decorating so he could help more people create beautiful places to call home with simple steps.

Matthew started blogging about Home Decorating Advice, DIY Projects, and Simple Decorating – Matthew now concentrates on what he is truly passionate about, showing others to use simple steps to creating and transforming homes into beautiful and meaningful places to call home regardless of the size of their budget.

Connect With Matthew

http://www.decoratingwithless.com/facebook

http://www.decoratingwithless.com/twitter1

http://www.decoratingwithless.com/pinterest1

Also, you can always write me at matthew@decoratingwithless.com and check out the blog at www.decoratingwithless.com.